GREAT AUSSIE CAR FAILS

STUFF-UPS AND STORIES THE CAR INDUSTRY WOULD RATHER FORGET

DAVE MORLEY

ONE OWNER
LOW MILES
NEEDS MINOR REPAIRS

Introduction

The development of the automotive industry has been a process of evolution and learning from our mistakes. But learn we did. Less than two decades after the first Benz Patent-Motorwagen spluttered around Karl Benz's backyard in 1885, Frenchman Louis Rigolly became the first man to drive a car at more than 100 miles per hour. Which must have felt like space travel back on 21 July, 1904 when it happened.

By the 1920s, Henry Ford had made the car an affordable consumer durable for American families, while Hitler's attempt to put a Volkswagen in every German household garage in the 1930s must rate as the least-toxic aspect of his grander plans.

Fashion grabbed hold of car design in the 1930s and beyond; ever since then, the story of the car has been one of the march of technology and the fine-tuning of a piece of equipment we now take absolutely for granted.

But like any epic journey, there have been plenty of one-step-forward-two-steps-back moments. Dreaming of a car is one thing; designing, engineering and selling it is another altogether. And it's that process that has so often and so spectacularly gone wrong. Sometimes Blind Freddy could have seen the problem brewing; other times even Nostradamus would have been surprised at the outcome.

Australia is no exception, of course, and while our now-departed industry was viewed globally as imaginative, flexible, efficient and resourceful, we were more than capable of cocking it up just as effectively and comprehensively as anyone else ever did. Which is what this book is about. It's a look back at the weird, loopy, inexplicable and just plain dodgy things that happened in six decades of making and selling cars here – and a few notable fails from other places, too.

Obviously, this book doesn't cover every mistake, tragedy and balls-up ... just the ones I can remember or was reminded of by the people listed on these pages. But there's one thing you can absolutely trust: everything you read here did really happen. None of it is made up, nor an interpretation on my, or anyone else's behalf. When you read it you'll understand, and be reminded of that great expression so often applied to all such moments of whoops: you couldn't make it up!

Australia has a proud history in car-making, except for some not-so-proud moments

Dogs I have known

CARS THAT WENT WRONG FOR ALL SORTS OF REASONS

HD Holden – it stands for 'hastily designed'

Every car maker has the odd skeleton in the cupboard; the model nobody ever talks about. For Holden, that car must surely be the HD of 1965. It didn't help that the HD was built between the EH and HR, a pair of Holdens revered by the masses and guaranteed to conjure the warm-and-fuzzies. But being the awkward middle child wasn't the source of the HD's woes.

The poor old HD was the victim of a design process that aimed to improve packaging, but attempted to do it on the cheap. To make the interior bigger, the designers moved the engine forward (for a smaller transmission hump) and then widened the whole body. Doing so without spending the money to do it properly created two problems. One: the forward-mounted engine cocked up the weight distribution, making the car understeer more than it should have. Two: the wider body was a nice thought, but Holden decided to plonk it on the same footprint as the physically smaller EH model. That meant the HD looked like its wheels were tucked way inside the wheel arches ('cos they were) and allowed the car to flop about in corners as the narrow front and rear tracks were a hostage to the physics involved.

But even that stuff paled into something approaching insignificance when you considered the HD's biggest flaw. Thanks to some inventive design work, the HD had those weird curves jutting out beside each headlight as

It looks great in the brochure, but this HD is probably already rusting

Aligning the headlights, or sharpening the kidney slicers (as the HD's bladed front guards became known)?

well as some truly complex metalwork to make even prosaic things like the door hinges work. All that creative metalwork required intricate folds and even joins where the complex shapes had to be made up of individual sections. And that, in turn, meant that the HD was really just a collection of rust-traps. First, the little nooks and crannies filled up with dust and leaves and whatnot, and then, the first time it rained, the water would be trapped in the gunk lurking inside the panels. Which then faithfully obeyed the laws of chemical reaction and started to rust.

Okay, so cars of the HD's era were often susceptible to the rust monsters, but the rate at which the HD decomposed was still startling. My dad bought a second-hand HD in the very early 1970s, so it was still a reasonably young car. But even by then, our HD was riddled with tinworm. The situation was made even worse by the fact that the rest of the car – the engine and gearbox, mainly – were borderline indestructible, so the car ran like a watch, but simply rusted out from underneath us.

Finally, Dad knew the time had come to ditch the HD, so the plan was to trade it in on a brand-new Holden in 1974 (a HQ). But what about the rust? Clearly, it couldn't all be fixed, but the boot floor was so full of holes something had to be done. So Dad's genius mate gave the floor of the boot a light malleting to shake the worst bits on to the ground. Then, he took some of that new-fangled fibreglass stuff and proceeded to patch the holes before giving the whole boot a quick (and thin) coat of underbody-black paint.

Dad recalls taking the HD to the Holden dealer to be valued for trade-in and making damn sure he parked the thing in the shade of a tree. Because if you opened the boot in direct sunlight, you could actually see your own shoes through the thin paint and translucent fibreglass. Ask yourself the last time you saw a HD Holden on the road. Now you know why.

In the interests of balance and fairness, the HD's design did incorporate one major advance: The lower-front door hinge was wide enough to support a large bottle of beer and still allow the door to be closed and hidden from sight. This turned out to be very handy in the pre-random breath testing days when the law turned up for a chat.

GIDDY UP

It's not unusual for a car company to use a critter as its emblem ... plenty have over the years. You're probably thinking of Holden's lion as a great example. But did you know that the first Holden emblem was not a lion at all? In fact, it was a life-size wooden horse that was nailed above the entrance of the Holden and Frost saddlery in Adelaide.

XK Falcon – overdue and underdone

Any importer trying to sell a car in any sort of volume in this country knows all about putting in the time to make sure it works here. We mightn't have autobahns, but we do have extremes of temperature and a percentage of roads that are not, by global standards, exactly up there with the best of them. It's why you see car makers now spending millions on taking a car that is right for just about anywhere else in the Western world and subject it to thousands of kilometres of specific testing here, and then invest millions more modifying the thing to get it to survive Down Under.

When Ford Australia began building the Falcon here in 1960, it was a mighty big deal. Twelve years earlier, Holden had begun production of the 48/215 Holden, and it had been a stunning success. Within a handful of years, every second car on the road was a Holden. Literally. Ford wanted a slice of that, so it invested heavily in a new production plant and head office on Melbourne's northern fringe, and then set about turning the US-market Falcon into a car that would sell here.

And sell it did. With more power than the Holden and a look that was 20 years ahead of the game, the XK Falcon should have carried Ford on its shoulders for years. Except Ford didn't do enough of that local engineering and testing we were talking about. The head honchos figured that what worked for North America would

Had the XK Falcon been any dodgier, we would never have had the fabulous Falcons that followed. Such as the XR model in the background.

work just as well down here. How wrong they were. So wrong, in fact, that the reliability disasters of the XK Falcon almost put paid to the whole Ford Australia experiment. It was t-h-a-t close.

Isn't 'disasters' a bit strong? Not if you've just bought a brand new car, only to have its front suspension fall in a heap a few weeks after driving it home to proudly show the neighbours. After just a few thousand kilometres on 1960s Aussie roads, the XK Falcon developed a nasty habit of allowing its front suspension to sag, leaving the car looking like a giraffe drinking.

The mounting points for the front-end were proving to be underdone for local potholes, and dismayed owners saw shock towers bending and cracking, as well as wishbones and shock absorbers bending. If that wasn't bad enough, plenty of XK owners experienced ball-joint failure, allowing the whole front suspension to collapse in a pile by the side of the road.

Forensic examinations soon discovered that the whole front structure was too weak and flexy, while the ball-joints were too small and weedy to cope with the pounding the cars were getting in the normal course of things.

Dogs I have known

Ford began running changes including braces from the firewall to the shock towers, and initially began offering the bigger, stouter ball-joints from the Compact Fairlane model as a fix. Not too surprisingly, just about everybody took up the tougher ball-joint option and, by 1962, the bigger units were being fitted to every car..

Unfortunately for Ford, the marketing damage was done with the whole project in danger of being zipped up and sent back to Detroit. But it wasn't, and that's largely down to local Ford engineers and management who saw the problem and did something about it. Even so, the Falcon's reputation wasn't really restored until the XP model of a few years later.

The point was that before the green button was pushed on the production line, better local testing would have spared Ford Oz all this corporate pain. Somebody should have realised that a car engineered for the smooth highways of North America might not cut it down here where potholes can bridge two parishes. Even if they thought it would survive, blokes in white coats should have tested that theory in the real world. But they didn't. They signed off on the thing too early and without any real idea what would happen next.

HANDY AT ANY SPEED

Keen petrol-heads will be familiar with the 'unsafe at any speed' US-market Chevy Corvair. But did you know that as well as the coupe, sedan, station wagon and convertible, there was also a commercial range? It's true. There was a windowless van (dubbed Corvan) and a microbus-style thing called a Greenbrier that could be had with up to eight doors. My fave, however, is the ute version, which came as either a Loadside (with a conventional tailgate) or a Rampside (with a side-loading facility). Why? Because, like the VW Kombi ute, the pancake motor under the rear made the load floor a bit higher.

... the marketing damage was done with the whole project in danger of being zipped up and sent back to Detroit.

The XK Falcon debacle acted as a warning to Holden. By the mid '70s, Holden was testing the German-engineered, European-market Opel as the basis of the new Commodore. And you better believe this was a big deal, because the new Commodore was going to replace the beloved Kingswood. So it had to be right.

Part of the process of getting it right was to take a bunch of prototype cars and a group of German engineers into the outback and flog the car in the name of durability testing. Much to the horror of the Germans, the prototypes began breaking in two, cracking where the boot met the rear window. They'd never seen anything like this. But here's the illustration of the cultural gulf between European and Australian car designers: While the Aussies were dreaming up ways of making the car stronger, the Germans' advice was to spend the money not on making the car tougher, but instead on making the roads better. They were probably only half joking. Suddenly, it was possible to see how Ford, led by the nose by Detroit, got it so wrong back in 1960.

The other great example was a range of cars from a variety of makers from the early and mid '70s out of Japan. These were the days when car makers were starting to embrace metallic paint and soft interior trim. Plenty of those Japanese makes and models, after a couple of years in the Aussie UV, went from pristine things of beauty to faded, scruffy-looking cars with split dashboards and interiors that had faded, cracked and generally come apart at the seams.

Holden Brougham – bad booty call

It took until the first BMW 3-Series of the mid-1970s for the concept of a compact luxury car to arrive. Until then, if it was a luxury image you were chasing, it was expressed by size. That explains why things like Rolls-Royces, Bentleys and Cadillacs had their own postcodes; if you wanted to impress anybody, you did it by physically outmuscling anything else on the road. Ever wondered why ancient cathedrals were so vast? It's the same theory: keep the peasants awestruck and they'll keep doing as they're told. Domination through intimidation.

But enough of the cod psycho-analysis. Having established that luxury car ground-rule, you can see that by making a car bigger in every direction you could maximise that effect. Which is why those big Yank land-yachts started to grow tail fins, got wide enough to seat four across the back seat and were longer than a weekend in Canberra.

Back here in Australia, both Ford and Holden started to look at those tanks. They realised you could charge a lot more for them despite the vast majority of components being shared with the bread-and-butter stuff, and figured they'd each have a dip at building a local luxo-barge.

Ford took the plunge first in March 1967. With experience of assembling the US-market Fairlane here since the 1950s, it hit the ground running with a stretched version of the 1966 XR Falcon

Holden's Brougham was luxury-car big. Just not where it needed to be.

sedan. Called the ZA Fairlane, the new prestige Ford got a more stylised front end with quad headlights, and a new rear end with square tail-lights and longer rear-quarter panels. Crucially, though (and this is important), Ford also did the smart thing and stretched the wheelbase of the big fella from 2819mm to 2964mm. All of that extra length was translated into leg-room in the rear, where there was almost enough space to stage a rodeo. Big blokes with big personalities absolutely loved the thing, and no racecourse car park was ever without a brace of Fairlanes again.

Holden, sniffing the air and smelling profits, was close on Ford's heels, releasing its own local prestige car just over a year later in mid-1968. Called the Brougham, it also had four headlights and a more stately view from the rear. Also following Ford's lead, it used more or less the same mechanical package as you got when you ponied up for your 1968 Kingswood.

But here's where it fell apart: instead of going to the effort of stretching the wheelbase, Holden simply tacked longer rear-quarter panels onto a HK Premier. So while it was longer than a Kingswood or Premier, all the extra length was hanging out behind the rear axle. True, that made for a huge boot, but it did nothing for rear-seat leg room which, even then, was the critical metric for this type of car.

Actually, by using the Premier (rather than the Kingswood) as the basis, Holden did at least manage to endow the Brougham with the squarer, more formal roofline of the Prem, which meant that headroom in the back was actually pretty good. But the other problem was that the thing just looked unbalanced and arse-heavy,

WE DID IT OUR WAY

I know we're all still reeling over the loss of our wonderful car-making industry, but it still amazes me at just how World War II accelerated our manufacturing in this country. The fact is that Australia built aeroplanes (Wirraways, Kangaroos, Wacketts, Woomeras and Boomerangs, to name just a few) long before it ever built a complete car. We also went from being a country that made virtually zero steel in 1914 to one making more than a million tonnes of it by 1939 as the war effort ramped up and it became clear that, thanks to our isolation, we were going to have to fend for ourselves in many situations.

Holden, sniffing the air and smelling profits, was close on Ford's heels, releasing its own local prestige car just over a year later in mid-1968.

and all the brocade trim, map pockets and cigarette lighters in the world weren't going to change that. Seems the buyers Holden imagined were too dumb to see through this ploy were, in fact, a bit more cynical than that, and knew fake news when they saw it.

The Brougham struggled along until the 1970s, trailing the Fairlane by a good margin in the sales race. Finally, with the launch of the all-new HQ Holden in 1971, the lion brand finally did the right thing and stretched the wheelbase to make a proper local prestige car. But you can bet they changed the name to avoid the new Statesman (and Statesman De Ville) suffering the bad rep of the Brougham's cheeky, nasty tacked-on booty.

Volkswagen Beetle – be very afraid

Everybody loves the original VW Beetle, right? Yeah, well, Herbie was actually a German double-agent in real life. He looked friendly on the outside, but scratch that beautifully painted surface and you revealed a chilling, homicidal maniac.

Look, I'm not going to try to tell you that the evergreen little Bug had no redeeming features. Because it did: it was well made from quality materials, it was a no-fuss solution to postwar transport for millions, it was reliable and great fun to own and drive. Until it tried to kill you.

I'll be charitable and say the design flaws were completely accidental and a direct function of the sort of technology floating around in the 1930s. But part of me also wants to remind you that the original Beetle's design was sketched under the stewardship of a certain goose-stepping German dictator. Make of that what you will. And let's not forget that the most endearing VW of all, the original Herbie, was dreamed up by Walt Disney, a man widely tipped to have been a fan of the way things were being done in Germany in the 1930s. However, enough of the conspiracy theories.

So exactly how was the VW Beetle planning world domination by wiping out the human race? Well, it started with the basic suspension. The original Beetle used what's known as swing-axles. These are, as the name implies, a

A VW Beetle sees out its last days in a paddock. Where it can't hurt anyone else.

pair of axles mounting the rear wheels that simply swing from a central pivot to allow the wheels to go up and down in that friendly, comfy, suspension-y kind of way. That was okay until the suspension started to lift (which is what happens when you turn a corner or hit a bump), at which point the rear wheels started to tuck under the car like the legs of a folding card table.

Then, when the Beetle fell back towards terra firma, the weight of the rear-mounted engine meant the wheels would be trapped under the car at weird angles. At this point, the suspension would try to stand the wheel up and fail, and the severely angled wheels would stay tucked under the car where they'd act as a ramp. With the help of all that weight sitting behind the rear-axle line, the car would get sideways, trip over its own rear wheel and that would send the rest of the car into a high-speed tumble-turn. This usually involved a rollover and, thanks to the Beetle's egg-with-headlights shape, often involved multiple somersaults until it hit something solid.

By the way, the Beetle wasn't the only car of the era with swing-axles: Czech carmaker Tatra also used this set-up and also had the (even heavier) V8 engine in the back.

Dogs I have known

After Germany invaded large tracts of Europe during that period of insanity we now refer to as World War II, its officers commandeered these Tatras as personal transport ('cos the Tatras matched their uniforms. Probably.). Things were dandy until Herr General tried to make it back to base in his Tatra after a pig's foot and a few steins of Krautlager at the wet mess after work. At which point, the Tatra would fall on its head at the first corner. In the end, the German high command had to ban its officers from the Tatra club, as it was calculated that these cars had killed almost as many German officers as Allied bullets ever did. Poetic, no?

Anyway, back to the VW psycho-killer. The other designed-in fatal flaws in the Beetle included a battery located under the rear seat. This was fine whilst ever being sat upon by small, lightweight bodies; but get a kid who'd been into the pies, and his or her kerb mass compressing the seat was often enough for the metal frame of the seat cushion to touch the battery terminals. Seriously - a wire seat frame that is able to come into contact with a battery and nice, dry, seat stuffing? Zippo couldn't have designed it better.

The first sign that all was not well would be the smell of burning seat-stuffing. That was usually followed by plumes of acrid smoke, and then the high-speed departure of the school-age pie-fancier. Since the Beetle was a two-door and Dad was still trying to work out what that weird smell was, Junior often exited the scene over Dad's shoulder. Sometimes Dad managed to stop the car beforehand. Sometimes he crashed the car nose-first into something in the process.

And this is where fatal flaw No. 3 comes into play. Because the Beetle

THEY WOULDN'T DARE ...

Heard the one about early Volkswagen Beetle hubcaps? The ones with the big, stamped VW logo on them? The rumour way, way back in the day was that, at a particular speed, the blurring logos on the hubcaps formed swastikas. Fear not, it's a furphy.

Seriously – a wire seat frame that is able to come into contact with a battery and nice, dry, seat stuffing? Zippo couldn't have designed it better.

was built back-to-front (with the engine in the back) everything that lives in the back of a normal car had to be mounted in the front of the Volksy. Stuff like the luggage and spare tyre and the tools. And the fuel tank.

Yep, although you couldn't see it, if the fuel cap was a bit iffy, you'd certainly smell the fuel tank as the fumes wafted back into the cabin through the speaker vent or the slightly open ashtray (can you see the problem there?). You could always tell when a Beetle had recently been filled up. Of course, Volkswagen was a tiny bit worried about this, so instead of having the fuel tank right at the front of the car where it'd be the first thing on the scene of the accident, the engineers moved it back as far as they could. Until it was sitting more or less in the driver's lap.

I've owned a stack (a fitting collective noun if ever there was one) of Beetles over the years and loved nearly every one of them. In fact, I still own one that, even though it was built in the 1970s, retains some of these, um, interesting features I've just mentioned. But mine's safe to use; I keep a clove of garlic and a crucifix in the luggage compartment. Right next to the fuel tank.

Leyland P76 – unready when you are

Uh-oh, here come the gags and the guffaws. Feast your eyes on the car that has become the poster child for getting it wrong. Yep, the Leyland P76 has been the butt of plenty of cruel jibes over the years and, to be honest, it deserved some of them. Frankly, the P76 stands as a lesson on how not launch an all-new car into a market sector already pretty well served by some old favourites.

The story starts in May 1973. It was all systems go, and Leyland Australia pushed the button to start production. And while the concept may have had some merit, the car itself was far from perfect in execution. That started with the way it was screwed together. Like its UK-based parent, Leyland Australia was having enormous difficulties at the time nailing quality control. A unionised workforce was not helping management's cause but, given what eventually happened to the Zetland plant in inner Sydney where Leyland production was centred, the union unrest ultimately did its members no favours, either.

More than that, though, the car simply wasn't right from the moment it launched. Even in those gentler times, when a few hours at the side of the road with a recalcitrant car was hardly the rarity it is now, the P76 was seen as unresolved in quality terms. The big complaints included doors that leaked air and, of course, dust; rear windows that simply fell out over bumps; and an

Mate, the boot can hold a 44-gallon drum. Who cares?

exhaust system that routed the piping so close to the floor that the optional carpets began smouldering. Interior trim items routinely jumped ship, and then there was the styling.

Leyland Australia had been made to lobby the UK parent so hard for the go-ahead to do a big car, there's speculation that it then felt the need to make it truly huge to justify its optimism. The old adage that the boot was big enough to fit a 44-gallon drum is actually true, but why that should be seen as a requirement for success is still being debated. Even by the standards of the time, the P76 is an awkward-looking child.

The wedge shape is apparent, but dubious, and the detail work seems misguided. It's simply too heavy in the rump to ever be called attractive, and that's pretty much that. That's despite the design being the work of Michelotti of Turin – a design studio that, among other things, had designed the very pretty Triumph 2500, the ground-breaking BMW 2002 and various Maseratis.

So how did a design by such craftsmen turn out so ungainly? Basically, the Michelotti design was fiddled with by Leyland Australia staff (perhaps on the instructions of their UK masters) who changed bits and pieces and demanded other parameters that completely diluted the purity of the original.

As the car aged (not that it had a particularly long innings) you could argue that the assembly glitches that characterised the finished product should have been fixed. But they never were. There was also speculation that the parent company, Leyland in the UK, was experiencing financial woes and couldn't fully fund the ongoing development of a project half a world away.

Against that background came strikes within the Leyland factory, and strikes within supplier companies that held up the parts necessary to finish cars. Many incomplete P76s wound up on grass at the factory, shy of the bits and pieces required to get them into showrooms. There was a steel shortage at one point, too, as the supplier involved failed to deliver the goods. Even power cuts hampered the P76's progress.

And let's not forget the fuel crisis that arrived just as the P76 hit dealerships. The launch also occurred at a time when both Holden and Ford were on the ascendancy. The HQ Holden, which was selling at the same time

Pretty soon, Leyland was changed to Laid-off

A P76 in the wild ... a rare sight these days

as the Leyland, went on to become one of Holden's most successful models with sales of almost half a million in three years. A tough act to follow.

There was political fallout, too. The federal government's Industry Assistance Commission reckoned there was room for three car makers in Australia, not four. And hot on the heels of the P76's demise, PM Gough Whitlam referred to it as 'a dud' and Bill Hayden famously called it a lemon.

Makes you wonder what chance it ever had ...

But to square things up a little, it's worth noting that the P76 did have its good points. Chief among those was that it was absolutely huge inside. There was plenty of headroom even in the back seat and the wide proportions made for lots of elbow and shoulder room. With the standard bench front seat, the P76 was a true six-seater. There was also exceptional vision to all sides, and only the high tail obscured the rear view for shorter drivers. And thanks to that 44-gallon-drum thing, the boot was simply vast and also featured a low loading lip and wide opening.

The body itself was clever too, and, despite the poor panel fit, was made up of just over 200 individual parts (allegedly only five more than the much smaller two-door Mini). This simplified production and made for a stronger bodyshell into the bargain.

The car drove well, too, with good brakes and positive steering. In fact, the driving experience was roundly praised by road tests that compared it favourably with its rivals. Fuel economy was also better than established players and the general view was that once Leyland got the build quality issues sorted out, P76s would fly out the door.

Of course, that never happened. Leyland never got the chance to get it right, because just 16 months later, in October 1974, the P76 project imploded, taking most of the Zetland plant and its employees with it.

VH SS Commodore – the faux Brockmobile

It's often observed that people enter a car showroom to buy the red convertible, but drive away in the white station-wagon. Okay, so the sensible station-wagon was the car they really needed in the first place, but the truth is that had it not been for that sexy red roadster, they might not have walked into that dealership at all.

It's called the halo car phenomenon and while it might be a niche market of its own when it comes to actual sales, it punches way above its weight in terms of how it makes people think about the brand generally. And whether they want a slice of that action.

A great example of this was the range of Brock HDT Commodores that were selling through Holden dealerships in the late 1970s and 1980. At the time, Peter Brock was a hugely bankable personality and, by having him build a line of bespoke Commodore-based road-burners, Holden dealerships would often be full of middle-aged blokes; a few reaching for their wallets and the rest dreaming and dribbling. It's that latter bunch that the halo-car deal was all about. Holden knew it was never going to sign them up for a Brockmobile, but it was equally sure the wannabes could be persuaded to splash out on a more affordable Holden. If you can't own the dream, at least own something like it, right?

But Holden jumped the shark in March 1982, just a few months after the VH model Commodore was launched.

If you can't own the dream, at least own something like it, right?

Among the many variants of the facelifted Holden was a new model called the SS. It was painted in the same shade of red as some of Brock's hand-built cars, used a V8 engine (admittedly the smaller 4.2-litre unit) and a manual gearbox, got similar alloy wheels to the Brockmobiles and even got a set of 'SS' decals that were identical to the ones gracing the flanks of a bona fide Brock car. All this, despite the SS being a straight production-line model that never saw the inside of Brock's Melbourne factory, that's for sure.

Even at the time, we all reckoned it was a cash-in by Holden (duh) but I don't recall anybody ever asking Brock what he thought about these faux HDT cars being offered at a much lower price than the real thing. I'm tipping he would have hedged his bets, figuring his deal with Holden was too sweet to jump on his high horse. Which is almost certainly why there was no fuss made at the time.

But just to prove that irony has a sense of humour, those stock SS Commodores are now worth a motza, purely because they were some kind of special-interest deal at the time. The fact that the VH SS was no more capable than any other VH SL with a 4.2 V8 and four-speed manual gearbox absolutely does not come into it. Actually, the same thing has happened to other decal-specials like the Holden Sandman, Monaro LE, Ford Falcon Cobra and Chrysler Drifter; all cars that were absolutely nothing special in their day, but are now worth serious money. If you can find one. And you know who the real winners are? The companies that are reproducing the decals in question.

Holden Piazza – the Gemini that won the lottery

Perhaps the kindest thing you could say about the Holden Piazza of 1986 was that it was arguably ahead of its time, offering a turbocharged engine in a hatchback body in an era when most hatchbacks were anything but sporty. Then again, when you looked at it critically, the majority of the Piazza wasn't exactly cutting-edge. The Piazza will be a real sporty hatch when a hot-dog-eating contest is a real sport.

You can't blame Holden for having a go with the Isuzu-sourced Piazza. It had done so well with the original rear-drive Gemini models that an upmarket, hatchback version with a flash turbocharged engine (the first turbo Holden, if you don't count the unofficial Country Dealer Team Gemini and Commodore turbos of a few years before) must have seemed like a good idea.

It might have been, too, if Holden had not got greedy with the sticker price, and the Piazza not been such an underachiever. The original sticker price was in the mid-$30s and after only a dribble of customers in the first few weeks, Holden took the axe to the price tag, reducing it to $29,000. In fact, so few had been sold that Holden was even prepared to write a cheque for $5000 to the handful of existing owners as a make-good for the tumbling resale value resulting from such a savage price cut. But even at 29 grand, you could buy the highly regarded VL Calais Turbo in the same Holden dealership for around the same money! Bzzzt.

Paint a Gemini with glue. Drive it through a $2 shop. One Piazza coming right up.

Looking at the Piazza in isolation didn't help. While the turbocharged engine was, in fact, electronically fuel-injected (as opposed to the old carburetted turbos around at the time) it made only 110kW with almost 1300kg to push around, so it was hardly a startling performer. That was probably for the best, though, because the Piazza handled like it was on casters.

The steering was lifeless, and a live rear axle was always keen to contribute its own input on which way the car should be facing. The brakes were underdone and, at any speed, the Piazza driver always had to consider the possibility they were pushing their luck.

The rest of the deal was just chintzy tat. That includes the semi-concealed headlights that made no sense then, or now. In fact, 'the Gemini that won the lottery' is probably the tag that will stay with me forever. And with the Piazza, too, presumably.

AU Falcon – why so sad?

There are people still working within Ford Australia who – if you direct them to a quiet corner, put a glass of wine in their hand and turn off your recorder – will admit to believing the AU Falcon of 1988 was the car that set the company on the path to closing up shop as a local manufacturer.

The launch of the AU was, they will whisper, the point at which the Australian car-buying public lost faith in the brand and the products it was capable of making. And this is despite the AU being one of the better Falcons over the years to drive, and far and away the most responsive and tactile to steer. Ever.

So how did it all go so wrong? Well, it started with Ford's new attitude towards fleet sales. For decades, the Falcon – with its big, roomy body and bomb-proof mechanicals – had appealed to fleets of all types and sizes. Taxi operators loved the thing for its hose-out construction, hire-car companies couldn't get enough of its rugged reliability and even police forces all over the nation were attracted to the Falcon's no-nonsense approach and a centre console that could hold two dozen doughnuts. None of which explains why, to mark the arrival of the AU, Ford Oz ditched a long-standing policy of heavy fleet discounts. It seems crazy, but that's what happened – even if there was no press release to say so.

This was doubly disappointing, because Ford's fleet customers were the ones who arguably would have been most likely to turn a blind eye to the AU's biggest – and ultimately fatal – flaw: that it was dingo ugly. Actually, that's not being fair to dingoes. Many families used to keep a photograph of an AU Falcon in a frame above the mantelpiece. It kept the kids away from the fire.

The droopy backside, the optimistically named 'waterfall' grille, the sad face, the domed roof, the skinny little wheels and tyres, the bulging flanks, the tippy-toed stance ... and that was just the outside. Inside, it was absolutely no better with a big, rounded centre-stack and lots of shapes Ford called 'organic'. Maybe they were right, because the interior surely stank. Okay, beauty is subjective, but that was certainly the majority view at the time.

While time dulls the pain of many an automotive howler, it remains a mystery how on earth somebody signed off on the AU's styling. At the time, Ford seemed a bit blind-sided by the controversy over the AU, but it still moved pretty damn quickly to try to put things right. That included bringing us a Series II car with more straight lines, and then a Series III version that featured even more stop-gap fixes. Eventually, though, Ford had to cave in and fast-track the BA Falcon, which still used a lot of the AU's tech but boasted a much more conventional appearance. Believe it or not, the BA even used the AU's roof and doors, so it's a credit to the designers that they made it look so different on such a tight budget.

What really stopped the whole AU thing from sliding into the swamp were Tickford-modified XR6 and XR8 versions. With their quad-headlight treatment and body kits to sharpen up the look, these were the pick of the bunch style-wise, as well as the best versions to drive with their stiffer suspension, lower ride height and improved engines. They should have gone on to become minor celebrities in the Ford world. But they haven't; they were still AUs, after all.

Mitsubishi Magna – off to a shaky start

On paper, the Australian-made Mitsubishi Magna of 1985 had it all going on. It had been re-engineered specifically for this market and, in design and packaging terms, was way ahead of the curve. In fact, it was only when mid-sized, four-cylinder cars emerged as real contenders more than a decade later that the Magna's potential brilliance was finally revealed.

But it wasn't all smiley faces back in the day.

Fact is, the Magna was a huge opportunity almost lost forever but it's worth back-tracking a little to see why it should have succeeded. That starts with the packaging, which was based on the Japanese-market Galant model, including the wedge-of-cheese styling that has dated pretty badly (it's not alone there). Somehow, the Australian arm of Mitsu managed to convince head office in Tokyo that the car needed to be bigger. Specifically, wider.

The green light was given for a prototype to be built involving more or less cutting a Galant down the middle and adding 65mm of width, as well as strengthening the overall package to cope with local roads. Don't forget the Magna, as the replacement for the much-loved Sigma model, had mighty big shoes to fill. But the plan this time around was to also go after Falcon and Commodore buyers, so interior space was king. It worked, too, and while the Magna couldn't match the Falcon for stretching room, it was at least as big (and slightly bigger in some directions) as the narrower VL Commodore.

The Magna was a winner in other ways, too. It was comfortable to drive, with a better level of ride comfort than its peers. And, compared with the wobbly old Falcon or a skatey, sketchy VL Commodore, the Magna was planted and felt secure. It was also quieter inside and just a more modern, resolved take on the whole family car deal. Downsides? Not many; mainly a lack of leg-room for the driver (the seat didn't travel far back enough) and a fair thirst for unleaded (for a four-cylinder engine).

But then it all started to unravel. First, there was a spate of automatic gearbox failures, and then engines started popping with worrying frequency. The problems ranged from warped cylinder heads to cracked engine blocks and, within a few short months, Mitsubishi dealerships got pretty good at dropping in new engines and gearboxes. And still it got worse; a batch of iffy con-rod bolts saw plenty of early Magnas throw a con-rod out the side of the block, trashing the entire engine in the process. Back to the dealership.

Just as Mitsubishi was getting on top of these problems, a few Magnas started turning up with rust forming in the roof panel. Oh dear. To be fair, most of these hassles had been eradicated by the time the facelift model, the TN, arrived in 1987. With the unveiling of the last of the first-shape cars, the TP in 1989, Mitsubishi had a truly sorted family car on its hands.

By then, of course, Ford had moved on to the dynamically improved EA Falcon (another car not without teething problems) and Holden had the vast VN Commodore in showrooms and was luring Aussie families back into cavernous, rather than generous, interiors. So, an opportunity blown? You'd have to say so.

Holden Camira – more snakes than ladders

Allow me to present a word-picture of the various power outputs of the Holden Camira's engine as it progressed through its troubled life. The new global mid-sized Holden started with an output of 63kW back when it was launched in 1982. Not great, but not terrible for the time. That figure jumped to 83kW (among the best in its class) for the JD model of 1984, but that all fell in a hole as unleaded petrol was introduced and the output from the same engine fell back to 64kW. The Camira rallied one last time in 1987 with the launch of the JE model, when power jumped back up to 85kW, but it was all too late. RIP Camira.

In fact, if you were to draw a graph of the power output of the Holden Camira's engine over the years it was on sale, the profile would be a bit of a metaphor for the whole Camira experience. From the highs of the initial expectations for the car that ultimately replaced the beloved Holden Torana, to the lows of poor quality control and sub-standard materials, the Camira was a wild ride. What finally killed the whole deal was that the snakes were always longer than the ladders.

In a way, the Camira is proof that the concept of a global car – one that is sold around the world in more-or-less singular form – is a nice idea, but one that doesn't always work out. In the Camira's case, what worked (in its Opel and Vauxhall forms) in Europe – where roads are smooth and car buyers are

A Camira, moments after the factory warranty expired

totally comfortable with front-wheel drive, manual gearboxes and peaky engines – was perfectly fine. But in Australia – where car buyers didn't trust front-wheel drive, didn't know how to drive a revvy engine, preferred automatics and where roads are often crapola – the Camira fell flat on its face in the mud.

Early adopters soon found that even though the Camira could get going, it really needed some dedicated thuggery on the throttle pedal to make it happen. The engine needed revs, and lots of them, to start making much power, and that just didn't compute with Aussie drivers. Also, the automatic transmission option – which had a big take-up rate here – was but a three-speeder and really hampered what you could make of that little engine.

The handling was less of a problem and, in fact, the Camira was quite tidy in corners with decent steering feel and accuracy, and an inherent balance that was all about good weight distribution and relatively advanced suspension. But front-wheel drive? Nope, that was still keeping plenty of buyers away. That only got worse as the Camira started to age and a few of them developed clunky CV joints in the driveshafts. Leading to plenty of I-told-you-so moments.

But even that wasn't as bad as the prevailing mood when early versions of the Camtech engine started developing premature wear and began smoking and burning oil. For a few generations of buyers brought up on Holden red motors with about three moving parts and a lifespan measured in hundreds of thousands of kilometres, this was just nightmare stuff.

Those early Camiras were also made of pretty thin steel, leading to a feeling of flimsiness, while rust got a decent toe-hold before some of them were even out of warranty. Hot spots included the doors, boot lid, front and rear windscreens, and even the firewall. A Camira with wet carpets also probably had rot in the front inner guards, allowing spray from the wheels to enter the cabin. The shonky metal also allowed the firewall to flex and crack under the forces imposed by the clutch cable as the car was being driven normally.

Inside was no better, with fragile plastics and appalling fit and finish. Tales of the roof lining falling in the driver's lap, the dashboard binnacle jumping ship, and the plastics cracking or crumbling were all common yarns down at the pub. Even the upmarket versions made you feel like you were sitting in lawn furniture.

Things started to look up a bit with the JD model of 1984 which got a bigger, 1.8-litre engine and a whopping (for the day) 83kW, suddenly making the Camira viable with the automatic gearbox option (although it was still a three-speed unit). But the rest of the deal remained, including the fly-apart interior and seriously dodgy build quality.

And then it all fell apart again as ULP came into being and Holden was forced to retune the Camira's high-stepping four-cylinder engine to cope with the new brew. Which is when output tumbled back to 64kW and, in the absence of any improvement in other areas, the Camira was absolutely back to square one. But it was four years older, and no longer the cute puppy of the Holden line-up.

Holden gave the dice one final roll for 1987 with the JE model, but we could all see that it was too little, too late. Even though the engine's fuel injection had been sorted out to cope better with ULP and the engine itself was now a full two litres, the JE was still plagued by sub-standard build quality and was now staggering around under the weight of the baggage of the Camira's

In a way, the Camira is proof that the concept of a global car ... is a nice idea, but one that doesn't always work out.

dreadful reputation. Even the stop-gap four-cylinder Commodore – itself a much-maligned piece of crap – was starting to look (slightly) less dubious when you parked its life story next to the Camira's.

Finally, after just on seven years of production and the incredible investment involved in building the Camira locally, Holden was forced to throw in the towel, axing the unloved Camira and wearing the loss and damage to the brand as a whole.

By then, Australia was knee-deep in the Button Plan which called for model-sharing among local car-makers as a way of making each individual model financially viable. So Holden replaced the Camira with a Holden Apollo-badged version of the Toyota Camry. In the process, it contributed to one of the great ironies of its corporate history: the car that replaced one of the least reliable Holdens ever was one of the most reliable Holdens ever. Except that it was a Toyota.

Ford Capri – timing (and quality) is everything

Ford got a whole bunch of things wrong with the Capri convertible it built in Australia in 1989, starting with the look of the thing. Somehow, it just never looked 'right' and with all those angles and the shovel nose, well, it was an unhappy collection of shapes to most eyes. But what else was wrong with the idea? How does a car go from great export hope to standing joke in less time than it was even on sale?

Let's start with the concept of making a car in Australia, based on a combination of Japanese and Italian engineering, for sale to North America. Okay, so the car was always going to be sold in Australia anyway, but a large part of the decision to build the Capri at all was down to the notion of selling plenty of them in the US. Thirty thousand a year, in fact. Which might have gone to plan had Ford not tried to sell the little drop-top through its Lincoln-Mercury dealerships. See, Ford dealers already had a Mustang convertible to shift, so there was concern that the Capri would meddle in that. But the Lincoln-Mercury division was basically a retirement home where people sometimes came in to buy a car. The only people under 70 who ever entered a Lincoln-Mercury showroom were looking for directions, not a two-seater convertible.

The Capri was also one of those car-by-committee jobs; styled by Ghia in Italy, the roof designed by ItalDesign (ditto) wind-tunnel testing by Fiat (ditto), structural testing in the UK and crash testing in the US. Talk about food miles.

But even that wasn't the end of the problems. Nope, you also have to lump incredibly bad timing into that mix. The Capri was launched at almost exactly the same time as the all-conquering Mazda MX-5, a convertible that has gone on to carve a place among the truly great cars of the last 100 years. All the engineering cues that marked the Mazda as something pure (rear-wheel-drive, north–south engine, brilliant steering) were also the very things the Capri was lacking. To drive the pair back-to-back (and we did, in the day) was to realise the Mazda was a classic in the making, while the Capri was a hatchback with the roof sawn off.

But possibly the Capri's biggest hurdle was the appalling build quality of the first cars to hit the market. Ford Oz was simultaneously struggling with big quality glitches on its then-new EA Falcon, so may have been distracted a little. Even so, the Capri's assembly quality was seriously off the pace. That was most dramatically illustrated by the fact that nobody could seem to get the roof to repel rainwater. Some Capri owners had their cars back and forth to Ford for anything up to three or four replacement roofs. And still they leaked. To be fair, Ford got partly on top of the quality deal late in the Capri's life, but it was all too late and the thing was already – and quite rightly – being remembered as a turkey.

The best thing to come out of the Ford Capri experience? A witty gag involving two engineers: one from Mazda and the other from Ford. The Mazda boffin is explaining his company's quality-control methods to his Ford counterpart: 'We randomly choose an MX-5 off the production line and place a domestic cat in the car before we go home at night,' he explains. 'Then, in the morning, if the cat has died, we know the car is air-tight and our quality is spot-on.'

Not to be outdone, the Ford white-coat offers his own method: 'We also randomly choose a Capri off the line and lock a cat inside at night. Then, in the morning, if the cat is still there, we know we've done our job properly.'

Hey, don't blame me, I don't make up the jokes.

Four-cylinder Commodore – a blueprint for failure

There's been a pretty simple line in the sand over the years: the Aussie family car needs a minimum of six cylinders under the bonnet. Eight is better still, but six is the least you can have before you'd open the lid to show the neighbours. Four cylinders? Nope, that won't cut it.

Mind you, this wasn't always the way. Back when cars were physically smaller, having a four-cylinder car as your family wheels was kind of okay. But Holden, Ford and Valiant established big cars with six-pot engines as the new normal.

None of which stopped Holden, with the advent of the VC Commodore in 1980, from unleashing possibly the biggest turkey since the Leyland P76. In fact, the four-cylinder Commodore was probably worse than the Leyland in most of the important areas and remains, to this day, a cautionary tale for other manufacturers.

The broad idea, in the face of mounting concern over both the price and actual supply of fuel, was to give Commodore owners a chance to make each litre take them a little further. Hard to believe now that the 1980 price-per-litre of about 30 cents was anything to get your knickers in a twist over, but anyway …

So Holden brewed a Commodore with 13-inch wheels and tyres (for lower gearing) and then turned its attention to a powerplant. Now, it could have brought in a proven four-cylinder

To drive the four-cylinder Commodore was to instantly understand that not all engineering is progress

unit from another manufacturer. There were some decent ones around, including a good one from Mitsubishi, and alternatives from Nissan, Toyota and even Mazda. But, no, Holden decided local content was the key, so it grabbed a 2.85-litre (173 cubic-inch) six off the production line, and reached for the angle-grinder. Or so the story goes. (I've also been told that the prototype concept engine produced by an outside company, once approved by Holden, was thrown straight into the nearest skip.)

Legend has it that Holden simply sliced the two rear cylinders off the six-cylinder block to arrive at the new engine, which bore the Starfire Four tag (quickly changed in schoolyards and front bars to Backfire Four). Of course it wasn't that simple (because all the oil would have leaked out) but the new engine did use the basic geometry (including the bore centres) of the old six, as well as sharing many internal components including the pistons. The crank had different phasing to suit the four-pot layout (ditto the camshaft) and the con-rods were beefed up to cope with the different stresses produced by a four-cylinder layout. All up, the engine made a fairly breathless 58kW and barely enough torque to defy a half-decent headwind.

And it was awful. Probably the only thing worse than driving the four-speed manual, four-cylinder Commodore was driving the three-speed automatic version. Not only were these things gutless, they had to be driven so hard that fuel consumption was barely any better than a six-cylinder Commodore. The other problem was noise and vibration, which the six-cylinder version already had in spades but was even worse in four-cylinder form. So there it was: it couldn't get out of its own way, was unpleasant to use and didn't really offer any fuel consumption (or any other) advantage. Game over.

A few strange observations have come out of the four-cylinder Commodore experience. The first is that Toyota – in an attempt to ramp up the local content of its range at about the same time – actually bought a batch of these horrendous engines and fitted them to its Corona model. Never an exciting car to begin with, the Corona was demonstrably worse as a result of this unwelcome gift from the accounting department.

The second is that Ford's rather excellent EcoBoost Falcon of just a few years ago still seemed to suffer from

The Backfire Four in all its breathless, gutless glory

The engine managed to ruin a perfectly good Toyota Corona, too

... it couldn't get out of its own way, was unpleasant to use and didn't really offer any fuel consumption (or any other) advantage. Game over.

the legacy of the underdone Holden, even though the turbocharged, four-cylinder Falcon hit showrooms more than 40 years later. With heaps of performance, great economy and probably the best Falcon chassis of the era, the EcoBoost deserved to do much better than it did. But the curse of the four-cylinder Aussie family car struck again.

And finally, in a world where everything eventually comes full circle, the all-new, imported Holden Commodore uses, in its volume-selling form – you guessed it – a four-cylinder. Yet even with 191kW of turbocharged power and a nine-speed automatic, it seems the buying public is still not ready for such a thing.

EA Falcon – a bit undercooked

By the time the 1980s drew to their power-dressing close, Ford's XF Falcon family car was older than a dad joke. After all, apart from a few minor twiddles (and a couple of bigger ones) the XF was not a radically different beast to the original XD Falcon launched almost a decade earlier. Not only that, but Ford would also have known that Holden had a brand-spanking new model waiting in the wings; a car not only powered by an exotic-sounding V6 engine, but one that would return the Holden family car to a full-sized format rather than the physically smaller design of the original Commodore. Back to the same size as the Falcon, crucially.

Clearly, Ford needed a new Falcon and the EA was to be that car. Problem was, thanks to that feeling of being cornered and needing to match Holden's on-sale date (or actually beat it to market, which it did by a few months) the EA Falcon wasn't fully cooked when it hit showrooms. You can see that in the way Ford saved time (and money) by using the rear section of the floorpan from the old XF model. That included the basic suspension, which amounted to a live axle and coil springs.

But the real still-frozen-in-the-middle stuff was evident in the automatic transmission (pretty much the default setting in Australia) that had been carried over from the XF. So, while the

New for 1988, the EA Falcon was as undercooked as the chooks seen here giving it the cold shoulder

new EA Falcon got a brand-new engine design with an overhead camshaft, it was tied to the same tired, old three-speed auto. Ford had its transmission supplier, BTR, working hard on a new four-speed auto 'box, but it simply wasn't ready in time for the planned launch date. A lot of car makers would have waited for the new automatic to come on stream before launching the car, but Ford wasn't that patient. It had to beat arch-rival Holden to the punch.

There were a couple of problems with this. First, the three gears in the old 'box were pretty widely spaced and didn't suit the way the new engine made its power. Those same ratios were fine in the old pushrod-style engine of the XF, which was more of a slugger. But the new single overhead cam (SOHC) engine was more of a revver and the old transmission simply didn't have the ratios to make that a harmonious arrangement.

Secondly, a four-speed automatic would have been a much more marketable proposition and looked a heap better in the sales brochure. Even worse, a four-speed auto was precisely what the new Holden was sporting. Not that the Holden's gearbox was a pinnacle of automotive excellence, but

Rushed to market to beat the competition, the Falcon EA was underdone and missing a gear

it was an obviously better thing than the EA's three-speeder.

The BTR four-speeder was finally production-ready in time for the first facelift (EA Series II) but the damage had already been done to the Falcon's reputation. And then, after a few months, the four-speed autos started to fail, too. The issue was eventually traced back to some harmful harmonics that were setting up destructive vibrations in the gearbox and causing failures. You can't help

... while the new EA Falcon got a brand-new engine design with an overhead camshaft, it was tied to the same tired, old three-speed auto.

but think that if BTR had had a bit longer to test the transmission in the context of the new Falcon, this might not have happened. As it was, some taxi drivers were swapping out the new four-speed auto for the old three-speed unit in the name of reliability. Not a good look.

So there was all of that. The other evidence to emerge that the EA Falcon needed more time in the oven came with the realisation that the paint quality was off the pace. That meant darker colours like deep reds, greens and blues were staring to fade and go chalky as the clear-coat literally fell off the car. Adding insult to injury, panel fit was iffy and many owners complained that their cars wouldn't hold a wheel alignment thanks to front ends that were a bit wobbly.

An all-new model often has what are politely called 'teething problems', but Ford's corporate teeth were now all over the floor like the aftermath of a pub brawl. Rushing a new product to market is never a great idea, and in the case of the EA Falcon, it probably put Ford even further behind the eight-ball than it should have been.

Ford Taurus – what a load of bull

Sometimes, you just have to wonder what the hell they were smoking in the boardroom. Take the Ford Taurus, for a prime example. Here was a car that was so hideously ugly, even the North Americans thought it looked weird. With a grille that looked like a deep-sea cod, and an overall shape that was similarly piscatorial, is it any wonder the thing floundered (sorry).

There wasn't a straight line on the Taurus (even the rear window was an almost-perfect oval shape) and there wasn't a good angle. If you squinted, it stayed ugly, but just got blurrier.

That was bad enough, but what on Earth possessed Ford Australia to lob the stinker into local showrooms? I mean, it wasn't like it was filling a market niche that Ford had previously ignored (unless you count pig-ugly four-door). Maybe it was seen as the ultimate sales challenge. I'd still have loved to have seen the look on the dealership sales manager's face on the morning the truck turned up with the first load of Tauruses.

See, the other problem - aside from the sheer homeliness of the thing - was that Ford already had a model called Fairmont Ghia that was doing pretty good business. So why put a similarly packaged car right beside it and price the pair almost identically? Doubtless Ford would claim it was simply giving customers more choice. But I can guarantee that 99 per cent of them

Last time you saw a face like that, it had a hook in its mouth

didn't take more than a millisecond to make that decision.

Aside from costing the same as the rather handsome Fairmont Ghia, the Taurus had a three-litre engine (versus a four-litre in the Fairmont) and wasn't as big inside. And for the conservative, older buyer that Ford was targeting, those looks were never going to stack up. Meantime, a Fairmont Ghia required absolutely no explanation at the RSL or the bowling club.

About the only real claim to fame the Taurus could manage was that its high-tech spark plugs only needed changing every 160,000km. Big deal. Especially when the thing disappeared after less than a year on sale.

EB Falcon GT – not so fast

Ford fans of performance motoring must have really felt left out of the loop in the 1980s and early '90s. Ford ditched the Falcon GT badge way back in 1976 after the XB version, and then, in 1983, went on to dump the V8 engine option.

While none of this was lost on the faithful – many of whom defected to Holden just to hear that V8 music – it also meant they were all ears when Ford announced not just the reintroduction of the V8 in the EB model of 1992, but also that it was striking another batch of GT badges for the same model. A new Falcon GT! What could be better?

Just 250 EB Falcon GTs were made in late 1992, and as well as a choice of only three colours (one of which was ultimately dropped as the Ford paint shop couldn't get it right) the body kit was way over the top for the early '90s. Organic shapes were clearly the in thing at Tickford in the day, and wheel-arch flares made a comeback with the EB GT.

Whatever you thought about the looks, you couldn't argue with 200kW of power that, at a time when HSV's Senator could manage just 180kW, was a mighty big line in the sand. Trouble was, the only EB GT that actually had all 200kW present and accounted for was the one in the brochures. Because when people started driving them, the performance didn't really mesh with what would be expected from a

200kW Falcon. Which inevitably led to independent dyno testing, and the discovery that Ford was playing pretty fast and loose with the numbers. The true output was probably closer to 180 or 190kW, but facts are facts and even if it's 190, it's still not 200. And let's not forget, Ford was charging $62,500 for the GT at a time when the bread-and-butter EB Falcon GL was in showrooms for less than 25 grand.

At the time, the hue and cry harmed the car's reputation and hung a bit of a cloud over the whole GT thing. Ford weathered the storm as did the EB GT which, thanks to its rarity and the GT badge, has gone on to become a very collectible car. And these days, when even hot-hatches have 200kW, the controversy surrounding the EB simply makes the car even more tantalising.

Which is not to say Ford failed to learn its lesson, because it surely did. In fact, there's a theory that it then switched to a policy of understating power outputs, most dramatically seen in the supercharged FG Falcon GS and GT models. With claims of 315 and 335kW respectively, it only took one drive to conclude that they were making quite a bit more than that. Maybe it was the memory of the EB GT furore, but more likely it was Ford reacting to the thought of the Fun Police steeping in if the actual outputs ever got out. But again, as far as collectors were concerned, the whole thing just made the cars even more desirable. Which they remain.

THE BAD OLD DAYS

We take safety for granted these days, but would you believe it was only in 1991 and on the EB Falcon that the big family car from Ford got a three-point rear-centre seatbelt? ABS was also an EB first but, typically, it was an extra-cost option back then. How things have changed, eh?

People-movers – 'cos people ain't parcels

When Toyota launched the very first version of its Tarago people-mover way back in 1983, it was a proper game-changer. And that was because that Tarago represented the first time a car-maker had really, honestly tried to make a people-mover that wasn't just a parcel van with extra seats bolted inside.

Sure, the original Tarago wasn't perfect, and still used a lot of components from the Toyota commercial-vehicle parts bin. But crucially, it got a trailing-link, coil-spring rear suspension (still a live axle, but hey ...) and that's what made it a bit special. Yes, you still sat right over the front axle to drive it. Yes, you still had to cope with a torsion-bar front end from the HiLux. But the rear suspension and plenty of interior modifications meant it didn't necessarily feel like a HiAce van to drive, or to sit in.

Now, a lot of people will be saying, hang on, what about the Volkswagen Kombi? Wasn't that the original people-mover? In many respects, yes, but when you look at the history and design of the thing, even those flashy Deluxe models with their little panoramic windows, roll-back sunroofs, stainless-steel trim and two-tone interiors were still based on the original one-box Kombi. And that vehicle was, without any quarrels, originally designed to move bread, flowers, and large lumps of dead animals. In fact, everything the average small-business punter needed to move in postwar Germany. Just not people.

... the only things in front of your knees were the headlight lenses and the big VW badge on the front. You were the crumple zone.

(And just in case you think I'm hating on all old air-cooled VWs, I'm not. I've owned several Beetles and Kombis and I've loved them dearly. It's simply that there were things about them that were just wrong. Funny-wrong, mainly, which is the point of this book, right?)

Anyway, before that time at Toyota, and way beyond that date for many other car makers, people-movers were awful things. The idea of bolting a couple of extra rows of seats into a parcel van was expedient, but made for a horrendous driving experience and absolutely compromised safety. Let's take our old mate the VW Kombi as an example of the latter. In the air-cooled Kombi, you sat with the steering column between your legs and about as far forward as it was possible to get without getting nose-prints on the inside of the windscreen. That meant the only things in front of your knees were the headlight lenses and the big VW badge on the front. You were the crumple zone. Your lungs were the airbags.

A lot of the Japanese contenders weren't really any better, placing you up high over the engine, but about as far forward as you could be. This was, of course, a hangover from the parcel-van design, where the engineers wanted the driver to take up as little space as possible to make room for more cargo.

That same credo was also responsible for the bluff front and slab sides that made the vehicle bigger inside, but also meant it had the aerodynamic qualities of a garden shed. So, those things were noisy at speed as the air blattering the front of the van tried to find a way past that upright front, and also unbelievably headstrong in a side wind. It was nothing to drive along in a Kombi with a side wind and have a full half-turn of steering applied, just to keep everything pointing in a straight line. The bigger danger was that you'd emerge from beside a truck or a billboard or whatever and suddenly cop a gust of side wind. At which point the bugger would dive for the shoulder (if you were lucky) or the centre line (if you weren't).

The Japanese brands had another nasty trick up their sleeve. Because they used the same crude suspension that was cheap to make and could carry a big load, they were dreadful to ride in. But worse than that, they were also possessed of iffy steering and a distinct lack of grip when you needed it most (in an emergency). Hell, some of them even retained the dual rear wheels of the parcel-van version which, along with stiff leaf springs and the tyre technology of the day, meant that they handled like a runaway fork-lift. The Ford/Mazda versions were probably the worst offenders, with so little grip that you couldn't park them on wet grass. Because you'd never get them moving again.

Hit the brakes in an emergency and the rearward brake bias kicked in, locking the rear wheels and sending the whole shemozzle even further

First Toyota Tarago is mostly only seen in wrecking yards these days, but it was a game changer. The other people-movers of the time were seriously crook.

out of control. Try to make a sudden steering input to get around an obstacle and the van would generally just carry on straight ahead, sending you directly into whatever fiery hell it was that you were trying to avoid.

The Kombi was better at this stuff thanks to its more compliant suspension, but even it had a parting shot – literally – just to keep you on your toes. Because of the way the engine was laid out with the carburettors towering over the distributor cap, any fuel leaks could easily start a fire that wasn't going to stop until the tank was dry. Even if the initial stages of the inferno killed the ignition and shut the engine down, you were still in big trouble because the fuel pump was driven off the engine, and the engine was still being turned over by the wheels. So fuel was still being pumped into the by-now raging engine-bay fire. Even this wouldn't have been so bad were it not for the design of the carburettors, which used a pushed-in fitting to get the fuel from the lines into the carbs. And guess what? These pressed-in fittings had a nasty habit of falling out thanks to time, heat cycles and vibration. All the things you got for free with an air-cooled VW engine.

People-movers are a lot better these days, with much-improved dynamics and, of course, safety. But when you look back at how it was, it's fair to speculate that the vasectomy industry owed a great debt of thanks to the unappealing nature of those early versions.

DANGER ZONE

On the morbid subject of the road toll, guess which country in the world is the easiest place to get wiped out on the road? If you said Libya, go to the fridge and get a beer, you've earned it. Yep, Libya will bury 73 out of every 100,000 people that drive or cycle on or even attempt to cross its roads and streets each year. Apparently, wearing your seatbelt is for wimps, and a zebra crossing is only for actual zebras.

Holden Adventra – when more is actually less

By the early part of this century, it was pretty obvious the world and its dog were over the idea of a conventional sedan or station wagon. For better or worse (don't get me started) the planet had gone completely barking mad for SUVs. And even if the jacked-up ride height, greater mass and compromised tyres meant that the S (Sport) part of the name was a complete joke, parking an SUV in the driveway was the new black.

Both Holden and Ford saw the writing on the wall and decided they needed to develop their own SUVs. Ford did the job properly, emerging with the rather excellent Territory. Holden? Well, it figured that if there was a shortcut to be had, that would do nicely.

That said, Holden obviously had big plans. Unlike Ford, which produced just the Territory on its all-wheel-drive platform, Holden managed to spin a dual-cab ute (Cross 8) off its Adventra station wagon and even gave the floorpan to Holden Special Vehicles to play with. In fact, HSV arguably did more with it, releasing its own versions of the Holden station wagon (Avalanche) and dual-cab ute (Avalanche XUV) as well as a Monaro-based Coupe 4 utilising the same all-wheel-drive system.

The all-wheel-drive system was borrowed from the US Hummer H2 program and was modified to work in Australia. It was no small-beer investment, either, with Holden spending around $50 million and making most of the bits and pieces itself, although the adaptor housing was sourced from the US. The set-up gave constant four-wheel drive which sent most of the torque to the rear axle. As has become the norm in SUVs, there was no low ratio.

In the end, all this extra hardware ruined the party. Even with revised front suspension arms, the extra driveshafts forced the Adventra's front wheels further out from the centre-line of the car. That meant Holden had to tack on a set of plasticky-looking wheel-arch flares, which did nothing for the already bulky appearance of the VY station wagon on which the Adventra was based. Meanwhile, those same driveshafts compromised the shape of the exhaust headers, so the engine in the all-wheel-drive versions actually made less power than conventional rear-drive Holdens.

Driveline packaging meant the only transmission offered was an old-hat four-speed automatic. The extra weight of the all-wheel-drive componentry not only made the Adventra pretty porky – weighing about a slab and a pie under two tonnes – but also decidedly more nose-heavy than the car it was based on. When the V6 version finally arrived some time after the early V8 models, that power-to-weight ratio went even further down the gurgler. Fundamentally, even with the V8 fitted, the sheer mass of the Adventra and its relatively low-IQ gearbox made it feel lumpen and doughy. Oh, and it guzzled fuel like a fighter jet.

The HSV stuff was no better, but the two-door Coupe 4 variant was probably the most adversely affected of all. Although it cost at least 10 grand more than a HSV-modified Monaro (the Coupe GTO), the Coupe 4 was slower, had less power, couldn't be had with a manual gearbox, drank more and looked pudgier. As they say in the classics, you didn't need to be Einstein.

Even Holden could see the writing on the wall, and it came as a surprise to precisely no one that the Adventra/Cross 8 concept never made the jump to the new VE Commodore in 2006.

Kia Rio Sport-Pac – the not-so-great pretender

'Tis said that imitation is the sincerest form of flattery, but Jeez, sometimes car makers take the piss. Take, for instance, the dreadful dealer-fitted, Australia-only option that Kia offered on the Rio sedan around 2005. Surely you remember it; it was called the Sport-Pac and it attempted to turn a Rio into a Subaru WRX. I'm talking front and rear wings, and even a Rex-aping bonnet-scoop (which didn't actually extend through to the actual engine bay, but anyway).

But what really put the Kia Rio Sport-Pac (iffy spelling notwithstanding) permanently on the Do Not Touch list was the way it shamelessly attempted to fool people that you were, in fact, driving a Subaru WRX. I'm talking about paint in that trademark STi shade of blue (almost, anyway) and a set of gold alloys.

Thing is, while the people who bought them went happily about imagining observers were admiring a WRX, the message they were sending out was the complete opposite. As in: 'I'd really like a Rex, but my mum/dad/insurance company/parole officer won't let me have one.'

You bought a Rio Sport-Pac for precisely the same reason kids in hoodies drive up and down the main street with the windows down and death-metal pounding: because nobody will let them into a nightclub.

In its natural state, the Kia Rio was a mostly harmless device ... but as an alternative to a Subaru WRX, they were more out of their depth than a federal politician at an integrity hearing.

In its natural state, the Kia Rio was a mostly harmless device that served a distinct purpose: getting kids to their first job or to uni, with a minimum of brain damage for dad. At that task, they were mostly adequate; but as an alternative to a Subaru WRX, they were more out of their depth than a federal politician at an integrity hearing.

At least you won't see one these days. Small mercy.

Wrecknology

TECHNOLOGICAL BLIND ALLEYS

Gull-wing doors: why?

Gull-wing doors on a car are a bit like driving around with a handgun in your glovebox – the idea sounds gangster-cool, but the reality might not be such fun when it all goes wrong. The problem with gull-wing doors is that once the novelty has worn off, they just add a whole lot of complexity to a car's design, compromise other bits, and make the whole shebang more expensive than it should be.

So why do it? Well, aside from the cool factor, gull-wing doors allow designers to add other elements that don't work with conventional doors. In the case of the Mercedes-Benz 300SLR of the 1950s, the top-hinged doors allowed the body to be stronger by making super-thick sills under the doors. With a conventional door, the high sills simply wouldn't have allowed a big-enough opening for the passengers to enter and exit the car. But by hinging the doors towards the centre of the roof and having the doors lift up vertically, a huge opening was available while still retaining the strength of that thick sill.

At other times, gull-wing doors have been found to be helpful on really wide cars with big, long doors that would otherwise need two parking spaces to allow the doors to open. With a gull-wing configuration that opens up and then out, the car can be parked much closer to solid objects and still allow passengers in and out.

Gull-wing doors: undeniably cool, but who really needs them?

Fundamentally, however, gull-wing doors are a waste of time and money and exist only to stroke the egos of those rich enough to indulge in them. They require some hugely complex hinge engineering and they impose a couple of incredible safety and ergonomic problems.

The first of those cropped up with the Mercedes-AMG SLS coupe of 2010. Aside from the cost and complexity of adding the gull-wing doors, the designers forgot one thing. And that was that when the doors were open, a passenger of average height was unable to reach high enough to close the door. I'm six foot tall in the old money and long in the body, and even I couldn't reach the door to pull it shut from the normal sitting position the seats place you in. The solution was to lift your backside up off the seat, make a desperate grab for the door and let yourself drop back into the seat, dragging the door – hopefully – down with you. One morning of running errands in the SLS and you were done with gull-wing doors for life. How rich but short people managed this feat, I do not know.

Then there was the Canadian-built Bricklin SV-1 of 1974. Although the Bricklin company boasted that the SV-1 was one of the safest cars on the road, that only counted while the thing was on its wheels. See, if you rolled the SV-1, it was impossible to open the centre-hinged doors as the weight of the upturned car would pin them shut. The AMG SLS got around this by having an explosive charge built into the hinges that would detonate if the car found itself upside-down, making it the first car in the world that could literally blow its own doors off. But the Bricklin? Not so much.

The most recent car company to realise that gull-wing doors might be more trouble than they're worth was Tesla. The brand's 2015 Model X SUV had rear doors that used a gull-wing design, paired with conventional front doors. So you could still escape an upturned Model X (through the front doors), but the Tesla's problem was a fit and finish one, and the company found that getting gull-wing doors to seal adequately was a huge hassle. Opening them after driving in rain could also deposit water onto the rear seat (and whoever was sitting there).

The Tesla gets around the problem of short people not being able to close the doors by having motors to open and shut them. But accounts from around the world suggest that sometimes

Huge gull-wing doors on the Tesla Model X have also proven to be a pain in the whatsit

Safe, until it was upside down at which point you were trapped

... gull-wing doors are a waste of time and money and exist only to stroke the egos of those rich enough to indulge in them.

these motorised doors have a habit of opening themselves. One door that opened itself was allegedly torn off a Model X by a passing truck, while other owners have reported the doors opening randomly at speed. All this after Tesla's effort to get the gull-wing door right actually delayed the launch of the entire car.

BLAME THE BENZES

Karl Benz might have invented the motor car but it was his wife, Bertha, who took the vehicle on its first long trip. In 1888, Bertha loaded two of her sons and some bratwurst sandwiches into the Patent Motorwagen and headed off on a 106km trip to visit her mother. So you can blame the Benz family directly for making it so easy to visit the mother-in-law.

Six-volt electrics: not enough of a good thing

If some is good, then more should be better, right? Exactly, and, unless you're strapped to an odd-looking chair in a southern state of the US, that's how it goes with electricity. And so it is that the latest car designs are shifting to 48-volt operation for some of their major functions, although the prevailing set-up is still the familiar solution where a 12-volt battery under the bonnet powers the car's major electrical systems.

But it wasn't always this way. Oh no. Back in black-and-white times, it was pretty normal for a car to use a six-volt battery along with six-volt globes in the lights, and a six-volt wiper motor (if you actually got electric wipers, and it was no gimme). Given that the battery and the car's systems were both six volt, it should have been okay. On paper.

In the real world, the six-volt electrical system blew chunks. Frankly, it just didn't have the grunt needed to start a car with a hot engine, or to power everything if you were running wipers, lights and heater fan all at once.

One of the things Ford Australia made sure of when it launched the first local Falcon, the XK, in 1960, was that the car had a 12-volt electrical system. Holden had already switched to 12 volts for the FE of 1956 (after nearly a decade of six-volt operation) so a six-volt Falcon was never going to cut it.

Probably the best-known popular car with a six-volt system was our old mate the Volkswagen Beetle. Precariously located under the seat where it could start a fire in the seat's stuffing, the Beetle battery was a six-volt job. Thanks to the small-capacity, low-compression engine, it managed to start the engine okay, but when it came to lighting up the road at night, the Beetle was pants. Those who remember reckon you had to get out and strike a match to see whether the lights were, in fact, switched on. Even with the VW's typically low cruising speed, it was always a car that could outrun its own headlights.

LET'S NOT START

Maybe you knew that the first production car to have an electric starter as standard was the 1912 Cadillac Model 30. But you mightn't know the sorry tale of how it came to be. Seems a good Samaritan named Byron Carter, way back when, stopped to help a female motorist restart her stalled car. But it didn't go well; the car backfired and the crank handle clobbered old Byron in the gob. He was taken to hospital with a broken jaw, which got infected and he died of gangrene. But he happened to be a personal friend of Cadillac founder Henry Leland, who vowed he would rid the world of this dangerous, crank-handle menace. The rest is history.

The floored design of early Holden utes

Boy, when those ducks line up, they really can crap on you. Back in the 1950s, many of Holden's Utility models had a tray floor made from a layer of plywood under a layer of Masonite. It was cheaper than using individual hardwood boards (like the timber floor in a house) and once you'd laid metal strips over the top of that, you had a decent surface over which to slide whatever it was you were carrying. It wasn't as good as a solid metal floor, but that was a lot more expensive to engineer and build. So a laminate of ply and Masonite was the go.

Here's where the first duck lined up: the tonneau cover for these utes was, as you'd expect, designed to keep the water out of the tray and off the load. Which it did while the car was brand-new; but by the time it'd spent a couple of summers under the Aussie sun, the vinyl tonneau cover had likely shrunk by a few millimetres.

Enter duck number two. Because Holden used a system of fiddly little metal clips rather than a nice stretchy, elastic rope that would allow for this small amount of contraction, once the shrinks had set in, it was virtually impossible to get the tonneau successfully clipped on again. At least, to the point where it didn't imitate a tent flap in a cyclone. So what did everyone do? They took the tonneau off and stashed it in a corner of the shed, didn't they?

Can you see duck number three coming? Yep, with the load area of the ute now lacking any form of

A pressed-wood floor in a ute. Not the best idea ever.

weather protection, it didn't take long for rainwater to inundate the two layers of timber sheet that formed the floor. And even though the floor panels were supported underneath by a series of metal ribs, once the floor had become wet enough, it could sag down between those ribs whenever you put a load of stuff in the tray. Sometimes the ribs themselves, after a few years of having wet plywood resting on them, would be pretty rusty and compromised as well, allowing for even more sag.

And now we come to duck number four: those early Holden utes used to store their spare wheel in a little drawer under the floor, accessed via a wee fold-down door under the tailgate. When you needed the spare – which was a lot more often in the old days of cross-ply tyres and crook roads – you opened the door and dragged the spare wheel out from under the floor. Which was fine, until you had the dreaded saggy floor and a load on board, at which point the floor would effectively trap the spare wheel under the weight of the payload. Stories of blokes having to shovel half-a-yard of gravel out on to the side of the road in order to get at their spare tyre were hardly unknown.

Before too much longer, Holden utes gained proper metal floors; although leaving the tonneau cover in the shed was still a problem, as water often got trapped in the corners and started the rust-monsters on their traditional path of destruction.

An idea that didn't suck – and that was the problem

Getting something for nothing is the holy grail of good design. And cars are no different. Making one component that can do two jobs or using a by-product of one operation to enhance another is about as good as it gets.

Modern hybrid cars that use the act of braking to recharge their batteries are a great idea and a great example. Braking energy that would be lost as heat and noise in a 'normal' car gets turned back into electricity and stored in the batteries for later use. Brilliant. The turbocharged engine is another idea that takes a by-product and turns it into something valuable. By using the exhaust gas flow from the engine (that would otherwise just disappear out the exhaust pipe) the turbocharger increases the power and efficiency of the engine. Like I said, something for nothing.

Now, one of the other by-products of the internal combustion engine is vacuum. The typical car engine is, if you break it right down, just an air pump, so this vacuum is a normal consequence. Car makers figured out a long time ago that they could use the force of this vacuum to provide power-assistance for the car's braking system. Thanks to that vacuum, you got a beautifully light brake pedal that could pull the car up smartly, rather than relying on the driver to develop a right thigh like a tree trunk to haul down a couple of tonnes of glass, metal and rubber.

But those same designers and engineers took a good idea too far when they invented vacuum-operated windscreen wipers. The theory was that the same vacuum that powers the brakes could be used to power the windscreen wipers. The wipers would no longer need an expensive, heavy electric motor to drive them and, since the vast majority of petrol car engines made vacuum, this stroke of genius could be applied to nearly any car.

In Australia in the 1950s and early '60s, vacuum wipers were the prevailing fitment to locally-made cars, but it soon became apparent that they were rubbish. How so? And why didn't they work when vacuum-powered braking assistance was such a Good Thing?

Fundamentally, the problem was that while all car engines create vacuum, they only do so when the car is either decelerating or just cruising along on a gentle throttle. And since you only apply the brakes (and therefore need the vacuum assistance) when you're decelerating, the vacuum brake-booster worked just fine. But wipers? Well, they need to work at any time, don't they?

The major flaw in all of this was that the vacuum wipers not only went on strike, they did so just when you needed them most. Let's say you're trundling along in the rain, stuck behind a slow-moving semi-trailer. Suddenly, the road ahead clears so you drop a gear, pull out from behind the truck and hit the throttle. Just as you start to accelerate into the wall of spray being thrown up by the truck, on the wrong side of the road, the wipers either slow to a crawl or stop altogether. Lovely.

How everyone failed to see this as a problem back at the prototype stage is the big question, although why some car makers persisted with this silliness for years is another pretty good one. Mind you, you get the impression the finance department might have had a fair bit to do with the relatively cheap technology outstaying its welcome.

In the end, vacuum wipers joined cross-ply tyres on the scrap-heap of automotive has-beens, and not before time. In other vacuum news, some car manufacturers stuck with the idea of using vacuum to produce other results. Some high-end cars used vacuum to operate both the air-conditioning vents and the central locking. Which is fine until the system ages and loses its efficiency – at which point you can stand beside a car for what feels like a lifetime while it gradually, and grudgingly, unlocks its doors after you've turned the key in the lock.

If ever vacuum truly sucked ...

Ergonomic disasters: the inside story

Ergonomics was just another four-syllable word to car designers back in the 1950s and '60s. By the time Ford started building the Australian Falcon as a means of toppling the juggernaut that was Holden, style was definitely being put before function in many areas.

Plenty of attention was being paid to interiors and that meant that the driving environment was often highly stylised, usually at the expense of function and, in some respects, even safety. Big, thin-rimmed steering wheels, often with chrome horn rings, were the norm, even though they were awful to hold and got hotter than a barbecue plate if the car had been parked in the sun. But they looked great, right?

The various switches throughout the cabin also fell victim to the style police. Both early Falcons and their contemporary Holdens tended to group their switches neatly together, usually down low on the edge of the dashboard. Again, this looked cool and lots of design time was spent making the actual switches look like little vases or trophies, just to complete the mood.

But that's where the problems started. Those vase-shaped switches were the perfect shape and in the perfect place to puncture your thigh in a shunt (and in the days before seatbelts, the dashboard didn't necessarily have to come to you). And the way the switches were grouped and the fact that one looked exactly like the next one meant that, say, going for the wipers as a truck sprayed the windscreen with mud in the middle of the night, often resulted in hitting the headlight switch by mistake. Oops.

It wasn't just lights and wipers that were the problem. Back then, cars had 'features' we don't see any more. Things like a choke lever and a cigarette lighter, both of which were placed with the rest with exactly the same-shaped knobs, just to make life more interesting than it already was on cross-ply tyres and drum brakes.

WHOOPS FM

We now take car radios for granted, but the whole idea nearly didn't make it. The two Americans trying to make the car radio concept workable back in 1929, William Lear and Elmer Wavering, had built a prototype and installed it in a Studebaker. They visited the local bank to get a loan to go into production, and decided to help things along by installing a spare radio in the bank manager's Packard. Some 30 minutes later, the Packard caught fire. No, they didn't get the loan. But the brand that they eventually established? Motorola.

FB/EK Holden's pillar of pain

You can see where Holden was going with the FB model of 1960. No, really. You only have to compare it with a 1957 US-market Chevrolet to figure it all out. Everything from the curved (domed) roof to the tail fins and the ornate, toothy grille all scream mid-'50s Americana.

But there was one design feature that Holden really should have ditched (not that the others weren't questionable in their own right). And that was the dogleg A-pillar that allowed the edge of the windscreen to wrap around the side of the car. Problem was, the door opening started before the windscreen stopped, so you wound up with this suspended chunk of metal and glass, right where any normal person would swing their leg to enter or leave the car.

I can tell you precisely how many owners of the FB (and the later, similarly styled EK) bashed their knee on this affectation: Every single one of them. At some point, that dogleg A-pillar would get you; either in the dark, when you were running late for a meeting, and sometimes when you were just trying to get in or even out of the damn car.

And that was the other part of the magic; the pillar would get you both coming or going. It didn't care. Common injuries included cuts, bruising, split kneecaps and also smashed windscreens (when, blinded by pain, you retaliated and smashed

All the two-tone paint in the world couldn't stop an EK or FB Holden from maiming you

whatever you were carrying into the glass).

Holden soon ditched the idea and, when the EJ Holden arrived in 1962, got a lot smarter. Instead of knee-traps, the EJ was there to help – the design is reckoned to have incorporated 37 places on which you could open a long-neck bottle of beer.

In 1962, that was giving the average dog some stiff competition as man's best friend.

PLATE DU JOUR

The first number plates to be displayed were in Paris, France in 1893, thanks to a change in French law to adopt the new system of identifying cars. The law was extended to the rest of France in 1901. And now we have everyone from toll road companies to speed camera operators and council parking officers watching our every move, courtesy of the humble number plate. Thanks for nothing, France.

Going fool throttle

I blame the marketing and styling departments of big car companies for lots of bad things. One of those is fake timber. But in order to understand how crapola fake wood is, it's important to understand what it represents.

Back in the old days, car makers – in the absence of much choice in materials – were kind of forced to resort to dead trees to build their cars. Originally, the whole frame of the car's body was made from timber. I once had a ride in a 1920s American Graham Brothers sedan and commented to the owner how tight the body felt for such an old girl. 'Yep,' confirmed the owner, who was sitting next to me, 'the weather's been pretty humid lately.'

Anyway, as technology and materials began their march forward, timber was used less and less. But one area where it was still popular, particular among luxury car makers, was for making dashboards. In fact, that's why it's called a dashboard; dash plus board. Geddit? An old Jaguar just wouldn't be an old Jaguar unless it leaked oil, refused to start every now and then, and had a polished walnut dashboard.

Problem was, in a decent head-first prang, that lovely solid timber dashboard turned into a thousand lethal punji sticks that basically skewered anyone in the front seat. That led to the invention of timber veneer, which was a wafer-thin layer of real wood that wouldn't break up and spear you

It doesn't look like wood, doesn't feel like wood and doesn't smell like wood. That's because it's plastic.

in a shunt, but still looked like a timber dashboard. Which it was, sort of.

Real high-end cars still, to this day, use timber veneer sliced off real trees; but, inevitably, some car makers wanted the look without the cost. Hello, fake timber. It's made from plastic or – sometimes – fibreglass with a faux timber grain moulded into it and coloured to resemble something a koala might sit in. That's the theory, anyway. The reality is that Keanu Reeves is way more wooden.

Thing is, the use of timber nowadays is a fairly unambiguous statement: I can afford to have my car built by craftsmen (or women), and you can't. But when you mass-produce a sheet of plastic to represent the same thing, that meaning is entirely lost on anybody with a functioning brain cell. And man, has it been applied to every kind of car – from a cheap sports coupe to the now-ubiquitous SUV. But regardless of what vehicle you apply it to, it's hard to believe it's fooling anybody. At all.

The most gloriously ridiculous misuse of fake timber – in this country anyway – came in 1962 when Ford launched the XL Falcon range. Within that line-up was a version called the Squire, which amounted to a bog-stock

Falcon station wagon with about four-and-a-half metres of fibreglass poorly disguised as timber tacked on to each flank. The broad idea was to play the nostalgia card by reminding us of the wonderful old US-market Ford 'Woody' wagons of the 1940s which really did have their sides made from hand-joined timber. But even the most gullible wouldn't have been taken in by the Squire's oafish attempt at deception. Oh, they're collectible these days, in much the same way as a World War I shell casing is a collectible; interesting now, but not something you wanted in your near vicinity back in the day.

The other, more recent, affectation that makes proper car guys roll their eyes is the dreaded fake carbon-fibre. Back in the 1980s when McLaren whipped the covers off its brand-new supercar, the F1, the big news was that it made extensive use of this new, high-tech carbon-fibre stuff. Until then, the mysterious, dull, black material was really only seen in Formula 1 cars and other top-secret military stuff. Suddenly, carbon-fibre was sexy and plenty of car makers went on to use it properly. But not everybody.

The big advantage of carbon-fibre was that it was, weight-for-weight,

Real Woody wagons were made from real wood

Here's what wood actually looks like

But even the most gullible wouldn't have been taken in by the Squire's oafish attempt at deception.

stronger than anything else anyone had ever built a car from. So you could make a very strong, safe car that was also stupidly light. And that meant more performance from the same engine.

So what do some car makers do? They use carbon-fibre for non-stressed bits of a car that have no need for it, other than to look expensive and exotic. This was selling this magnificent, genius material way short; but worse was to come.

Indeed, it wasn't long before some overworked designer – doubtless channelling the work of the inventor of fake timber – came up with fake carbon-fibre. Within a few years, the horrible stuff was plastered across dashboards, seat inserts, centre consoles, steering wheels and even exterior mirrors. In fact, anywhere that real carbon-fibre could be wasted in a non-structural area, now the fake stuff was taking its place.

Getting into deep shift

I'd be lying if I said I know how or why the column-shifted manual gearbox came about. In the very beginning, manual gearboxes were floor-shifted, which makes all sorts of sense as the shifter simply bolted to the gearbox's selector levers and then poked up through the floor above the gearbox. But somewhere along the line (the late '30s in America, I believe) some marketing type decided this was all too gauche and that the modern lady or gentleman would much rather shift gears by pulling and pushing a lever mounted on the steering column. And bingo, the three-on-the-tree was born.

Actually, by the time full-sized Australian cars came along, there was a tangible benefit to the column-shift; you could get three people across the front bench seat and not risk being locked up for fiddling with the centre passenger's nether bits when all you were trying to do was shift into top. Which is probably why column-shifts existed at all, even though Harvey Weinstein hadn't been invented yet.

Anyway, there was a generation of Holden family cars – from the late '60s and early '70s – that had a column-shifted manual as the default setting (floor shifters were reserved for the souped-up, performance models) but were complete bastards to use. They weren't so bad when the cars – the HK, HT and HG models – were brand-spankers. But get some wear in the long linkages, joins, pivots and elbows that joined the shifter to the gearbox's selector levers – via the engine bay, if you don't mind – and you suddenly had a mega-tangle on your hands.

When this convoluted set of metal rods and split-pins decided to jam up, you were guaranteed of not being able to select a gear – any gear – from neutral. Which was less than tragic if it happened in your driveway, but was far more likely to occur while you were facing a fresh green light after you'd been sitting at the red in neutral. At which point, tragic barely covered it. The only solution was to open the bonnet, get out of the car, lean into the engine bay and manually untangle the linkages from each other. And ignore the tooting horns, waved fists and shouted obscenities of those stuck behind you.

Another Aussie car to have a drama with its column shift (for a completely different reason) was the early Valiant. These also had a three-speed manual gearbox and, to give the linkages a straighter shot at the selector levers, those levers pointed down from the side of the gearbox, aimed straight at the ground. That made them one of the lowest points on the car. Which was fine until you ran over something like a dead kangaroo (still a relatively common thing to do in regional Australia) and the ex-marsupial could actually smack the selector rods and cause the gearbox to simultaneously select not just one, but two gears.

Now, without going into the physics of gear reductions and such, I can tell you that selecting two gears in the one gearbox at the same time is a lot like jamming a broom handle through the spokes of a pushbike – everything stops, and it stops fast. In some cases in these Valiants, that would involve the back wheels locking instantly, sending you into a skid that may or may not have carted you into the mulga. Thanks to the way the driveline was laid out, even pushing in the clutch didn't get the wheels turning again.

More often than not, though, the gearbox, under the intense forces inside, simply blew apart like a hand grenade. Hot oil and tiny bits of metal would litter the road as you clattered to a stop, hoping like hell that somebody would hurry up and invent the mobile phone so you could ring a tow-truck. 'Cos otherwise, my friend, you were walking home. Apparently, nobody went broke in those days selling floor-shift conversions (which positioned the linkages pointing up) for Valiants.

How the Pinto engine got camshafted

Fiddling with a car in your driveway on a Saturday morning is not the simple matter it once was. Electronics, with their inherent evil and treachery, have ruined this once lovely pastime. But back in the day, it was great fun to mess around with your car and convince yourself you'd made it faster.

Plenty of car makers used to make it even more fun by building engines that were simple to work on and super-tuneable. One of the best of them was Ford's 2.0-litre four-cylinder unit, dubbed the Pinto on world markets. This little powerhouse went into every kind of Ford, from hot-rod Escorts to Transit vans, and served the blue-oval brand very well over the years.

Forget four-valves per cylinder and electronic fuel injection; the Pinto used a carburettor and a single overhead camshaft. But the basic design was so sound that you could tune it up easily, usually starting with adding a second carburettor. The engine also responded well to a change of camshaft and you could go pretty wild in the cam department in something like an Escort; because the car was so light, you could trade off a bit of bottom-end grunt for some more revs and power up high. Which is where a lot of tuners went hunting, and wound up with cars that were fast (for the time) and gangs of fun to drive.

The only problem with a camshaft change in a Pinto, however, was in the way the camshaft was fitted to the engine. In most single-overhead camshaft designs, the camshaft itself can be removed either from directly above or from the front of the engine. That is, by removing the radiator and maybe the grille, you have enough room to slide the old camshaft out of the engine bay before slotting the new cam in its place. And all the while, the rest of the engine remains in place. Lovely.

But for reasons known only to Ford's engine designers, the Pinto's camshaft could only be removed from the rear of the engine. So, it was either tear out the dashboard, cut a hole in the firewall and withdraw the camshaft through the glovebox from inside the car; or remove the cylinder head with the cam still in place, change the camshaft on a bench and then bolt the head back on. Which, of course, is what everyone did, cursing and damning Ford's engineers all the while. Maybe the idea was dreamed up by the company that produced Ford's head gaskets, because its stocks sure as hell went up as a result.

Somebody will one day figure out how many otherwise-productive man hours were wasted by this foible, but since I can't recall a Ford Pinto that hadn't been backyard-fiddled, it'll surely run into the millions.

BLAGGER'S CHOICE

We all know the Jaguar Mk 2 was the motor of choice for London's East End villains in the 1960s, but figures from the Met (London's police force) suggest the real blagger was the Ford Transit van. In fact, the Met estimates that 95 per cent of armed robberies in the UK in the 1970s involved a Transit. And you suspect the figures for burglaries and other robberies would have been just as high. You wouldn't have found those figures in the van's sales brochure, though.

HQ's fuelish filler

If your job is to produce paintings or sculptures or diamond-studded tiaras, placing form before function is unlikely to end your career. After all, such things exist purely for their form, and the fact they can't double up as a coat-rack or a letter-opener is of little or no consequence. But you can't get away with the same caper when it comes to car design. Nope, even if it looks fabulous, if it's going to make the end-product vehicle less user-friendly or less convenient or less practical, then you need to be prepared to bone the dashboard-mounted Statue of David and cancel your order of diamond-encrusted gear knobs. Either that, or it's Centrelink for you. Not all car designers have recognised this.

Back in the late 1960s – a point in history when the average Holden buyer thought aesthetics were bum exercises – Holden was working on making the new-for-1971 HQ model a sleek, stylish piece of work. It mostly got there, too, with the aggressive grille and headlights and the slim A-pillars that remain a positive lesson to car designers around the world. But in one important area, Holden allowed form to dictate terms to our old mate function. And that was hammered home to every HQ Holden owner, not just the first time they tried to refuel the car, but every other time after that for as long as they owned the bastard thing.

See, what Holden had tried to do was to tidy the appearance of the car

Hiding the fuel cap is a way to clean up a car's look. Hiding it behind a number plate as low as the HQ's was an equally good way of making that same car impossible to fill.

and give it smooth, sexy flanks. And that meant hiding the fuel cap. Now, most car-makers, when pursuing the same level of detail, usually elected (and still do) to hide the fuel cap behind a hinged flap. Not Holden. Nope, it decided that the only place to put the fuel cap was behind a hinged panel that mounted the rear number plate. They might have gotten away with it, had the rear plate been placed higher on the back of the car. But since the HQ's boot swept down and then curved over (that style thing again) the number plate was recessed into the low-mounted rear bumper, between the tail-lights.

So even with the fuel tank itself mounted low under the floor of the boot, the angle of the tube between the opening where you stuck the nozzle and the actual fuel tank was very slight. Now, even the dimmest plumber knows two things: Thursday is pay-day, and turds roll downhill. So that same plumber would have been able to advise Holden that placing the filler neck so low on the car meant that the path the fuel needed to follow was not steep enough. In fact, it was shallow enough that fuel being pumped in would inevitably slosh and gurgle and burp back up the filler pipe where it would force the bowser to 'click off', on average, 50 times per filling session. Imagine trying to pour water uphill and you're getting the idea. It was worse if the car itself was pointing even slightly uphill, as now the angle was even less. And the fuller the tank got, the more contrary the operation became.

So fuelling took longer than it should have done. Big deal. Well, yes, but as anybody who has ever attempted the feat will tell you, that same low filing point at the back of the car meant you had to perform this drawn-out procedure pretty much in the downward-dog position in order to operate the pump trigger. And this, remember, was decades before the invention of yoga pants. Your other option was to fill the car from a kneeling position; undignified and hard on the knees, but this did at least place you in the correct position to whisper a quick prayer to the gods of polyester clothing (and there was a bit of that about in the early '70s) that your eight-inch shirt lapel wasn't about to throw a static-electricity spark at the same moment the petrol gurgled back up the filler neck and splurted out all over you.

Just to add insult to (preventable) injury, once you'd paid for your fuel and got going again, the sloshing action caused by pulling back into the traffic was enough to send fuel cascading out the filler neck, and past the ill-fitting lockable petrol cap that was such a popular option back then. Good times.

BUNGED UP

When Ford started making the Mark II Escort RS2000 locally, it soon became obvious that the piddly fuel tank from the 1.3 or 1.6 wasn't going to give the range the thirstier two-litre needed. So Ford did the only sensible thing and fitted a bigger fuel tank, with the filler behind the number plate. Which meant the filler cap on the right-rear quarter was redundant. But did Ford press a new quarter panel? Nope, it fitted a plastic bung instead! Cheap, or what?

In fact, it was shallow enough that fuel being pumped in would inevitably slosh and gurgle and burp back up the filler pipe where it would force the bowser to 'click off', on average, 50 times per filling session.

Illusions of grandeur

The idea of a high-performance coupe isn't new; Bentley has been doing it for years and years, right back to the Continental R models of the 1950s. So it was no real surprise when Ford Australia had a dip at the concept in 1973 with a car called the Landau.

The Landau was essentially an XA Falcon Hardtop with all the chintzy shit-and-glitter of the LTD luxury sedan. That included some truly bizarre interior fitments, as well as those vacuum-operated covers for the headlights. And it also included a set of the biggest, heaviest hubcaps you've ever seen. Seriously, these were monsters, and the rumour back in the day – and it was almost certainly true – was that if one of the hubcaps copped a knock, it could send the whole wheel-and-tyre package out of balance and put a shimmy through the entire car.

Apparently, the solution was to balance the wheel, tyre and hubcap as a single unit and then make sure you put the hubcap back on in the correct position when you re-fitted the wheel. Now that's taking style too far.

Check those hubcaps. You don't get many of those to the kilo.

The Landau's styling was heavy-handed. But, like chopper push-bikes, all the kids want one now.

INSPIRED IN THE USA

We love to think of our classic Holdens and Fords as uniquely home-grown, but when you look more closely, you can see a lot of US design inspiration. Okay, so we all know the XK and XR Falcons were Australianised US designs; but on a subtler level, have you ever seen a Ford Torino Hardtop parked next to an XA or XB Hardtop? The similarities are striking. And what about the ever-popular steel rims on a HQ GTS or SS (and optional on other HQs)? One look at the rims on a 1970 Pontiac Firebird Trans Am and the truth is revealed.

The problem with the Hemi six

There's one sure-fire way to ensure an engineering project will have the odd problem or two. And that's to start the development program with one team of engineers in one country, half-finish it and then send the project to another team of white-coats in another country half a world away. That's exactly what happened with the Hemi six-cylinder engine that powered Aussie Valiants in the 1970s. It (probably) explains why there was one major oversight in the engine's design.

The project to design and engineer a brand-new inline six-cylinder engine started in the US in the mid '60s when Dodge decided it needed a new large-capacity six to replace the old slant-six in its range of Dodge trucks. But somewhere along the line, Dodge lost interest and the whole project was in danger of being stuck in a filing cabinet and forgotten.

At the same time as Dodge was shelving the new six, Chrysler in Australia was looking for a new big-six to replace the Aussie version of the slant-six in its passenger cars. So the half-finished engine was shipped to Chrysler in Adelaide and the final development and design work was carried out there, leading to the 245 and 265 Hemi sixes that became the strong, dependable and grunty engines that went on to power Valiants, Centuras and the fabulous Australian Chargers.

But while the engine was a great thing in its day, there was one element of the design that was simply forgotten about. And that was a method of preventing the camshaft from 'walking' or moving fore and aft. Since the oil pump was driven off the camshaft via helically-cut gears, that led to drag that tried to make the camshaft move backwards and forwards in its bearings. In turn, that prompted the ignition timing (which was also driven off the camshaft by another set of gears) to vary according to where the cam was located at that moment. And it only got worse as the engine (and the timing chain) started to get a bit of wear in it.

Our bush mechanics soon came up with a solution, which was to insert a little screw-adjuster in the timing cover which poked into the engine and bore on the camshaft when you adjusted it properly. That effectively stopped any fore-aft movement in the camshaft; and while it sounds a bit primitive, it's actually a very satisfactory solution. The big question, though, is how on earth two teams of grown-ups managed to miss this fairly important element in an engine's design.

The little screw-and-lock-nut deal addresses the designed-in flaw in a Valiant six-cylinder engine. But how'd it get past the engineers in the first place?

Piston broke? Try some Ajax

The 1970s was a time in Australia when medium-sized four-cylinder cars were really starting to catch on. It was the Mitsubishi Sigma (early versions were actually badged Chrysler) that led the charge and managed to make family-car buyers think twice about traditional full-sized six-cylinder cars.

The Sigma's success led to an onslaught of new models from both Europe and Japan, with even the local manufacturers adapting older designs to a four-cylinder future and Holden developing its own home-grown four-cylinder powerplant (which you'll read about elsewhere in this book). Ultimately, it was the Japanese makes with their value-for-money advantage that ruled the roost with models such as the Datsun 200B, Mazda 626 and Toyota Corona all selling strongly.

In the process, they introduced a whole generation of car buyers to concepts such as standard carpet, air-conditioning and a floor-mounted gearshift. But equally, they really took some liberties in quality terms. Especially once Aussie families started using them as true replacements for older, bigger cars and expecting the same sort of performance and longevity from them.

One of the big problems facing both Datsun and Mazda was poor engine life. Even though these were physically big 2.0-litre motors, they seemed to be underdone in some important ways – mainly in the design of, and materials used in, their piston rings. Datsuns could start to become oil burners before 100,000km had passed under their wheels, and the Mazda 626 was even worse. You could often smell a 626 coming before you could hear or see it. And following one was easy; just keep your eye on the trail of blue oil smoke.

There are many causes of oil burning in car engines but in the case of this pair, the trade has filed it under soft piston rings, rather than any inherent design fault or flaw. Which, even in the 1970s, was crazy stuff; we'd been mass-producing the internal combustion engine for almost a century by then, yet here was a couple of mass-market manufacturers unable to master the basics.

The problem of the too-soft rings was that they'd wear out fast and then lose their tension, reducing their ability to control the oil in the engine. When that happened, the oil could get past the rings and into the combustion chamber where it was burnt (leading to the smoke and smell). If this happened for long enough, the engine would eventually consume all its lubricating oil and come to a grinding, terminal halt. But this piston-ring wear was also matched on the surface the rings moved on; the walls of the cylinder would lose their textured surface and become smooth, making the problem even worse.

If all this seemed silly given that the technology was well known, well understood and totally mastered by other companies, then the fix was even crazier. They wouldn't admit it at the time but car dealers, faced with an irate customer whose too-new car was burning oil, sometimes made a not-so-difficult choice. They could either rebuild the engine, which would cost real money, or they could try a little trick that sometimes slowed or even stopped the engine's oil-burning habits (for a while, anyway ... usually just long enough for the car to run out of factory warranty). And that trick was to start the engine, remove the oil filler cap and shake a good handful of Ajax into the engine.

Say again? Yep. The bathroom-sink cleaning Ajax. The science was pretty simple: the abrasive cleaning powder would go through the engine and remove the glaze (the shiny surface) of the cylinder walls by scuffing it up on its way through. Anything left went straight out the exhaust pipe and, if you used enough Ajax, the car would stop consuming its own lubricant. Or at least make it drink less of it on a decent run.

It sounds pretty crude – and it was – but when you think about it, it kind of replicated the process involved in giving an engine a cylinder hone, which is what a proper workshop does to fix glazed bores. Except the Ajax method didn't involve all that pesky disassembly, cost and labour. Strangely enough, Ajax never included this usage on its packaging.

The vinyl roof: a belly laugh waiting to happen

If there's ever been a less-subtle automotive accessory than the vinyl roof, then I don't think I've ever come across it. Except maybe for a gadget trialled in the 1970s that attached to the dashboard, rolled a cigarette for you, lit it and then set the rest of the interior on fire. Irrefutable proof that smoking can, in fact, kill you.

Anyway, back to the vinyl roof. Maybe you can guess what would happen if you stuck a large patch of vinyl to a sheet of tin and left it out in the weather. Yep, moisture would eventually migrate between the non-breathable vinyl and the metal, get trapped there and before you knew it, you'd have a nice little rust farm on your hands. What's amazing, then, is that nobody ever applied this same logical flow chart to car making.

Which is, I guess, how some cars – notably in the 1970s – left the production line with a vinyl roof. It is also precisely how those same cars, just a handful of years later, had bubbles starting to form under the vinyl, making it look like coloured bubble-wrap. I'd like to think some owners tried to hammer the bubbles flat with something heavy; but if they did, they'd have probably smashed through the whole roof panel, clobbering the poor sod in the back seat, because those bubbles were actually little rust monsters.

The only fix was to remove the vinyl covering, then the glue that was now

The padded, half-vinyl roof with opera windows, thy name is kitsch

several years old and harder to shift than a rent-protected tenant, repair the rust holes, panel-beat the roof back into its original smooth shape, and then paint the roof.

So how did the vinyl roof ever come about, given that it added cost to the car, reduced its durability and – in the majority of cases, certainly in hindsight – made the whole thing look tacky? Well, some folks back then just liked the look of two-tone cars. And that's the effect you could get with a vinyl roof. It's also an effect you can manage just by painting the roof a different colour to the rest of the car on the production line (which is what used to happen in the 1960s), without the side effects.

But here's how you just know the whole vinyl-roof thing was a belly-laugh waiting to happen: the real, original, honest-to-goodness idea behind the vinyl roof was to soften the shape of the roofline and make the neighbours think you were driving – wait for it – a convertible. No kidding. Some North American-market Fords even had a huge, fake hinge stuck to the C-pillar to further the lie that the car was a drop-top.

The only thing worse was an affectation called the half-vinyl roof which, as the name suggests, involved covering just the rear half of the roof in vinyl. This was intended to suggest a landau roof (look it up), a la olde-worlde chauffeur-driven cars where the driver and his (and it was always a fella) passengers sat in totally separate compartments. Which looked pretty stupid on a four-door family car. Don't know about you, but they weren't fooling me.

Yes, folks, that's a fake hinge; intended to further convince you this is a convertible

BATHED IN A GREEN GLOW

Taking the lead out of petrol was a pretty good move in the name of public health and safety. But would you believe that in the 1950s, Lancia (for one) was still using uranium in its cars? It's true. The cars weren't nuclear powered, but the lenses of the driving/fog lights on some Lancia B20s certainly did contain some uranium. The inclusion of uranium gave the lights a weird green glow, even switched off. Turns out the lenses were made from what's known as uranium glass and, as the name suggests, was a material containing trace amounts of uranium (as an oxide) mixed into the glass before moulding. Somewhere around 2 per cent uranium was used in most cases. Apparently, the radioactivity of uranium glass is negligible, so the substance was even used in tableware and household items from 1880 to about 1920.

... the real, original, honest-to-goodness idea behind the vinyl roof was to soften the shape of the roofline and make the neighbours think you were driving - wait for it - a convertible.

Tyred and emotional

Ever wondered why a lot of 1970s and '80s European cars – such as some BMW, Audi, Mercedes-Benz, Citroën, Peugeot, Ferrari, Alfa Romeo, Renault, and Saab models – have aftermarket wheels fitted? It's not that the original wheels were toad-ugly or anything; it was all the fault of the tyre industry. Specifically, it was Michelin that caused this trend, but did so with the best intentions.

Back in the '70s, Michelin designed a new style of tyre with a stronger bead (the bit that joins the tyre to the wheel) that allowed for a radial tyre with higher performance and improved ride – which is kind of the holy grail of tyre technology. However, the redesigned bead also meant that the new tyres, dubbed TRX, wouldn't fit on a conventional wheel rim, so Michelin took the step of designing both the tyre and the rim to suit it. So far, so good.

But the compromises soon started showing up. Just for starters, the new tyre design confounded tyre shops, whose machinery no longer worked as well on these new Michelins, which were physically very difficult to remove and fit. Also, to differentiate the new TRXs from 'ordinary' tyres, Michelin made them in metric sizes where every other tyre maker in the world had agreed years ago they would make tyres in imperial sizes. (Doubtless the American tyre industry had a bit to say in that decision.) So even if you could have made the TRX

Eventually, many car owners realised it would be cheaper to buy a set of aftermarket wheels and somebody else's tyres than a new set of TRXs.

bead fit a conventional wheel, the two components were incompatible on size in any case.

What happened was that owners of TRX-shod cars were soon looking for replacement tyres and discovered they were locked into buying expensive TRXs. Eventually, many car owners realised it would be cheaper to buy a set of aftermarket wheels and somebody else's tyres than a new set of TRXs. Extra salt was rubbed into that wound when the rest of the tyre industry caught up with the TRX in terms of performance, and Michelin lost even that edge.

It wasn't only Michelin that fell into this trap (although it was by far the biggest maker of metric tyres). Following Michelin's lead, tyre brands including Avon, Continental, Goodyear and even Dunlop made limited numbers of metric tyres for specific makes and models

Needless to say, metric tyres haven't made a comeback since. But the aftermarket alloy wheel industry absolutely loved this period in automotive history.

Emission control, we have a problem

The first of July 1976 is kind of a black day in Australian motoring. No, it's not the day petrol hit a dollar a litre, nor is it the day Ford axed the 351 Cleveland. Nope, what made that date one of the darkest hours for Aussie car buyers was a little acronym called ADR 27A. The ADR part stands for Australian Design Rule which is a set of strict guidelines and regulations to which car makers are obliged, by law, to adhere. The second bit, 27A, was just the number assigned to this new piece of legislation.

So what made ADR 27A so terrible? Fundamentally, the intention of the new design rule was good. It aimed to clean up the emissions of new cars, both through reduced tailpipe emissions and from the evaporation of fuel from the tank and the rest of the fuel system. Believe it or not, back in 1976, it was quite common for fuel to evaporate either through the fuel cap or the various vents and breathers in a car's carburettor (Australia was a still a fair way from fuel-injection in '76).

Tackling the evaporation problem usually involved fitting a better fuel cap and a charcoal canister that caught and trapped the fumes evaporating from elsewhere. Not such a big deal. But the tailpipe emissions angle was tackled by forcing the engine to consume a certain percentage of its own exhaust as a means of burning more of the fuel and air it contained. A second time through the processor,

Of all the local manufacturers, Chrysler probably tried hardest to make new-for-76 emissions controls work

if you like. The problem was that by swallowing some of its own exhaust, there was now less room in the engine's cylinders for fresh fuel and air (which burned much better). So, inevitably, performance dropped.

But it was worse than that. Because the engine was trying to burn a less-volatile mixture, the ignition timing had to be backed off and, in some cases, compression ratios needed to be dropped. Both things led to engines that ran rougher, were harder to start and ran hotter, all while making less horsepower. In turn, that meant driving them harder, which used more fuel and kind of negated any tailpipe emission improvement. Ah well.

Interestingly, Australia's car makers didn't necessarily see eye-to-eye on what was the best way around all of this. Chrysler gave its otherwise-thirsty V8 Valiant models a clever ignition system and carburettor combination. Dubbed Electronic Lean Burn (ELB), the system allowed the ignition to call some of the shots and adjust the carburettor on the run, reducing fuel consumption. It used a complex network of vacuum lines, causing a lot of mechanics to throw their hands in the air. But road tests in the day claimed that the big six-cylinder

Valiants (ELB was extended to the sixes in 1978) could beat 10 litres per 100km on the highway – and that was really saying something at the time.

Ford also had a decent crack at making ADR 27A less evil than it already was. It did so by developing a new cross-flow cylinder head at a significant cost to the company. But it worked – sort of – because the new engines didn't suffer too badly in output terms and remained pretty civilised. It would have been nice to drive a Falcon with the new cylinder head that wasn't consuming its own exhaust fumes, though, and see just how much better it would have been. Lots, probably.

Sadly, it was Holden that really dropped the ball when it came to making its locally-made engines comply with 27A. Unprepared to invest in better technology, Holden just left the old six-cylinder and V8 engines to suffer at the hands of the new rule. And suffer they did. They all suddenly made a lot less power, ran hot in many cases and drank even more fuel. And they were no sippers previously. We began hearing stories of people who'd traded their old HQ for a cleaner new HX, only to find that it would no longer climb the big hill on the way home without

CREATIVE GENIUS

Creative interpretation of the rules is a time-honoured process in motor racing. And pretty much nobody was better at it than the late Harry Firth. Harry designed the Ford Cortina GT in the '60s to win at Bathurst, but the rules in those days stipulated that the car must run as it was delivered off the showroom floor. So Harry dictated that Ford dealers delivered the GT500 with the air-cleaner in the boot, allowing the car to run with an open carb at Bathurst. Must have been something in it, because a Cortina GT won at Bathurst in 1965.

Unprepared to invest in better technology, Holden just left the old six-cylinder and V8 engines to suffer at the hands of the new rule. And suffer they did.

overheating. The very same hill that the traded-in HQ with the 'same' engine used to glide over. In fact, so bad was the power drop-off that Holden, for the HX model of 1976, actually dumped the entry-level 2.85-litre six from the catalogue, as it simply wouldn't have been able to move the car sufficiently to see off a fat kid on a push-bike.

Of course, it wasn't just the Aussie car makers who had to deal with ADR 27A. Imported cars sold here also had to comply, and there were all sorts of engine-driven air pump systems and exhaust gas valves developed and tried. Some of them worked better than others, but most of them actually hampered the production of horsepower.

To this day, you'll still hear people praising the merits of a pre-1976 car over its later counterpart, purely on the basis of ADR 27A and the havoc and heartache it caused.

Velouria

Back in the 1980s, nothing screamed luxury car quite like an interior made from that fuzzy velour stuff. And in the decade before that, it was probably brocade trim that made the same statement. But the truth is that both materials were about as functional as a chocolate teapot.

Let's start with brocade. Some samples of this stuff have been dated back to the Middle Ages and it was popular with royalty and the rich and famous. It looks almost like a piece of cloth has been embroidered with a pattern, but it's actually the result of the weaving technique. Either way, by the time it's had a couple of big bums sliding over it as a car seat a few hundred times, it can start to look pretty tatty. Holden was perhaps brocade's biggest fan in the late '60s and early '70s and the brand's Brougham luxury sedan was the major recipient.

The next step along the evolutionary path towards well-intentioned interior decorating was velour. This furry, staticky, man-made (usually polyester) material is designed to give you the warm and fuzzies but, in reality, the carpet in a third-rate Las Vegas casino is likely to look more natural. Aside from attracting every stain and dust mote on the planet, early velour was also pretty delicate stuff.

Local car makers used it to give an impression of plushness and luxury in their upmarket cars, but European and

Hard to believe velour trim was ever cool. Then again, it was the 1980s and Madonna was still singing 'Like a Virgin' without blushing.

Japanese car makers wanted in on the velour act as well. The problem there was that those same interior designers had never experienced an Aussie summer or the UV radiation levels that go with it. The result was an interior material that faded in the first year and then completely exploded in year two, spilling its stuffing-guts all over the rest of the interior.

In more modern times, the use of Alcantara on steering wheels runs brocade and velour a close race for dopiest interior material ever. While Alcantara (fake suede) feels lovely, it can't be wiped clean and absorbs every drop of sweat and ounce of grime that human paws introduce to it in the everyday act of driving the car. Give an Alcantara steering wheel a year and the World Health Organization will be slapping a bio-hazard sticker on your car.

It's all bad news for cows, though, because any of these materials make leather trim look like a work of genius.

Won't get tooled again

Amortisation is the name of game in car making. The term refers to the process of making production equipment a better investment by building more and more cars with it. With each car produced, the per-unit cost of that investment gets smaller and smaller until you reach break-even point. At which point it's happy days. Happy, profitable days.

But you can overdo it. By trying to make too many components from the one set of equipment (known as tooling in the car biz) you risk the quality of those components failing. And that's because the tooling itself wears out. Seen a kitchen knife worn down to almost nothing after decades of carving the Sunday roast? Or a slate step worn down by a thousand generations of people walking on it? Same thing. And if the tooling is worn out, then the components it produces will also be out of shape or an incorrect size. When it comes to engine components, where measurements of hundredths (and even thousandths) of a millimetre are the rule rather than the exception, any wear in tooling is bad news.

Back in the 1980s, Holden stretched things a bit too far with the tooling that made some of the really intrinsic bits and pieces of its six-cylinder engine. The Holden six in question was the second-generation inline six, first seen in cars in 1963. Over the years, it progressed through various different capacities, but one thing hadn't really changed; the tooling it was made with. So it's no surprise to hear that by 1985, the tooling was well and truly worn out, having turned out parts for literally millions of engines.

Not that you were going to hear that from Holden and, with plans to replace the locally-made six with an imported engine (from Nissan, of all places) for the next model, Holden figured it would just keep pumping out the old engine and not let on that it was producing some truly bad examples. To get around this, cylinder blocks straight out of the foundry were being hand-measured and then matched to a set of pistons that were the best fit. Flaws in the casting process were also a problem, with the cylinders not always ending up precisely where they should have been (it's called core-shift). Plenty of crankshafts were showing up with the wrong-sized journals, too, so over-sized bearings were being fitted.

The problem was made public when one of the state motoring clubs bought a brand-new Holden for one of its executives, who immediately complained that his new Commodore was using oil and making rattling sounds from under the bonnet. The club's engineering department stepped in and soon hypothesised that even though the car was brand new, the engine was so loosely built that it had the tolerances of an engine that was just about ready to be replaced through old age. Having decided that, the engineers then checked their hunch by ripping the engine out, tearing it down and carefully measuring every component. And yep, what they found was a new engine that, thanks to that worn tooling, was right on the edge of the maximum wear limits (tolerances) specified by Holden's own blueprints.

They contacted Holden and asked for a response. Holden gave them one: it simply rewrote the document on tolerances to bring these worn-out engines back into the black. That, however, was of no use to the people who had already bought brand-new cars with engines that had factory-fitted wear.

The first (EH) and last (VK) models to use the old-faithful Holden red six

Digital dashboard dramas

Around the mid-1980s, Holden, Ford and Mitsubishi started messing about with digital dashboards. And messing about is the right description, because in pretty much every case, the end result was a classic dog's breakfast.

The idea was sound, and experience has shown that modern dashboards, some of which use a 100 per cent computer-generated image, can work. Even back in 1987, the idea was that these displays would be more reliable than the old cable-driven stuff, more accurate and offer more information while reducing the cost to the manufacturer. The main problem was that they were just downright difficult to interpret on the move. The speed readout was often a flickering series of numbers as the vehicle's velocity altered. On the Ford Fairmont Ghia version in particular, one little bar graph looked awfully like the next.

Still, full marks for attempting something new and anticipating a trend, because modern digital displays, with their ability to tailor a view to a particular situation, are absolutely brilliant. Need to navigate to somewhere new? Then call up the satnav screen as your main display and receive other information on a need-to-know basis. Fancy a racy, high-definition cluster that shows everything from lap times to G-forces in real time? Yep, modern dashboards can do that, too. But these early versions? Not so much.

Early digital dashboards were an exercise in illegibility. Even the cool, single-spoke steering wheel couldn't save this Holden Calais.

The real issue was that they didn't really give any new information that an old analogue dash didn't. But at the same time, they were borderline illegible in some light conditions, or at speed when you really had to read, rather than just glance at them (which is the mark of a poor gauge layout, regardless of what technology it uses).

What was perhaps most interesting about the end results from the three manufacturers was that they were so similar in the way they attempted to convey some important information. They all had a numerical readout for speed, for instance, and each one used a bar graph to display engine revs. They were also universally difficult to read, fiddly and a backward step from a well-designed conventional display with good old-fashioned needles and dials. Oh, and they also had a tendency to go 'Phut!', permanently and expensively.

The sorry tale of Brock's Polarizer

There are a thousand ways to ruin a perfectly good relationship. Just ask any marriage counsellor. But in the curious case of Peter Brock and Holden, the relationship that was torn apart in 1987 had been so good for both parties up until then that it was just about unthinkable that what we were watching was a very public, very messy divorce. And it was all kicked off by a little box of optimism called the Energy Polarizer.

Back in the day, in the office of the car magazine I was working for, we managed to obtain (don't ask me how) one of the infamous Polarizers. Unable to contain our curiosity, we prised the lid off the little grey box and eagerly peered inside. Frankly, we wound up none the wiser. Inside, encased in resin, was what appeared to be a magnet wrapped in silver foil, with a couple of thin wires coming out from it.

But whatever the Polarizer was supposed to be (and there were lots of claims) the grey plastic box was the catalyst for probably the ugliest automotive stoush this country has ever seen. Not only did it spell the end of Peter Brock's HDT road-car empire, it killed off his factory-sponsored race team. It also drove a wedge between Brock himself and Holden, the very company that had done so much to nurture Brock and create the legend that still surrounds his memory. And it really shouldn't have happened.

But whatever the Polarizer was supposed to be ... the grey plastic box was the catalyst for probably the ugliest automotive stoush this country has ever seen.

It all started in the mid-1980s when Brock, at a low ebb physically, sought the services of a healer. He began to see Dr Eric Dowker, a chiropractor who taught Brock about the healing power of crystals as well as an arcane branch of 'science' known as orgone energy. Orgone energy is, supposedly, a natural force that can be harnessed with crystals and can align molecules in solid objects. The Polarizer, said Brock, was a way to tap into that energy and align the individual molecules of a car, turning a shithouse car (his words, not mine) into a good one.

Sounds a bit sketchy? Well, there was plenty more where that came from. The Polarizer was required to be fitted under the bonnet of the car, against the firewall, and it wouldn't work without the 'antenna', which amounted to a Polarizer sticker usually placed on the rear window.

Conservative old Holden wasn't best pleased. Without some solid science behind this little gadget, there were corporate concerns that the company was opening itself up for a legal broadside if anybody ever proved the thing didn't live up to Brock's claims. There was no real thought that the Polarizer might provide any negative results. But the thought that, through a Holden dealership, HDT's customers could be paying (about $480 back in the day) for something shonky that did nothing at all sent Holden's top brass into trembling spasms.

Wrecknology

Brock himself? Well, to talk to him at the time, he clearly believed in his gadget. Enough to start insisting that only customers who ticked the Polarizer box would get the great man's signature on their car. And it got even crazier as Brock, sensing Holden's unease, began moving the antenna decal from the rear window to the bootlid, where it was hidden by the rear spoiler.

Suddenly it was solicitors' letters at 10 paces. And we all know how it ended.

Actually, there's plenty to suggest that the Polarizer was really the last straw in the Brock-Holden bust-up. Rumours at the time suggested Holden was pretty jittery about what Brock was supplying in terms of the modifications he was making to his road cars. The fear was that Brock, when asked for a little extra by his cashed-up customers, was making modifications beyond those listed in the brochure. And in an age where the Feds were getting serious about emissions and safety standards, that was never going to fly. For Holden, the thought of getting caught up in a legal spat involving potentially iffy cars being sold through its dealerships and

Brock's Polarizer. Proof that if you don't want the genie, don't rub the lamp.

The man. The legend. What Polarizer?

carrying a Holden factory warranty was a scandal too far.

That theory is supported by the fact that the whole thing came to a head one night in February 1987, at a convention centre in Melbourne, when Brock and Dr Dowker pulled the wraps off a car called the HDT Director. Based on a VL Commodore, the Director had several contentious elements, including an independent rear-suspension system that Holden had not been able to test for durability, and a standard Polarizer, which Holden had, by now, tested and declared a big old nothing-burger.

If you really want to get all cloak-and-dagger about it, the Polarizer was heaven-sent, as it allowed Holden to throw Brock under the bus without looking like the bad guy. And since Brock's claims for the Polarizer were failing the pub test on a daily basis, that's precisely how it panned out.

Ultimately, Brock worked his way back into Holden's favours and the whole relationship was patched up. But the old expression of 'easy to forgive, harder to forget' was never truer.

BANNED AND PROUD OF IT

You kind of know you've made it in motorsport when you get banned. That's what happened in NASCAR to the glorious Dodge Charger Daytona back in 1970, after it blew the opposition out of the water and broke the 200mph barrier (322km/h) for the first time on a track. NASCAR moved to ban all aero cars as a result. The Daytona's close relation, the Plymouth Super Bird, suffered the same fate.

EA Falcon's smashing innovation

Sometimes, the pace of technology can outrun the people who fix our cars. A classic example of this occurred in the late 1980s when Ford pulled the wraps off its brand-new EA Falcon. Suddenly, the old XF Falcon was so yesterday it wasn't funny, and the EA's overhead camshaft engine and steering rack replacing the old car's steering box was dead-set spaceship stuff.

But there was another improvement the EA brought with it over the XF, and that was in the science of fitting the front and rear glass to the car. In previous Falcons, the windscreen had been surrounded by a big rubber seal that extended right around the edge of the glass. When that seal was stretched and popped onto the metal lip that formed the windscreen opening, bingo, the windscreen was officially in place. Until a passing truck threw up a dirty great rock and broke the bugger; but you get the idea.

Meantime, the new EA used a clever system of actually gluing the glass to the car, making the whole structure stronger by making the front and rear 'screens part of that structure. Without the small degree of movement allowed by the old-style rubber seal, the bodyshell had less flex and the new Falcon was stronger. And safer. And by using the glass as a stressed member (to use an engineering term), Ford was able to reduce the size and mass of other parts of the

Sometimes new technology just means new problems. Early bonded windscreens were a great example.

roof structure and still have sufficient strength to prevent the roof caving in if the worst happened and the Falcon wound up on its lid.

The problems started when EAs began turning up with broken windscreens (due to the normal causes) and went to windscreen shops to have new glass fitted. While some fitters were up to speed with the new glue-in process, a lot weren't, and in some cases the wrong grade or type of adhesive was being used. If that happened, you could wind up with a car that looked fine and didn't leak; but if it was in a shunt, it wouldn't have the proper degree of strength to keep the passenger cell from collapsing in on the hapless occupants.

There was no way of knowing whether the correct adhesive had been used just by looking, and as EA Falcons started to hit the second-hand market, it all become a bit of a lottery. Provided you could trace the repair history of a particular car, you could be pretty sure you were okay; if not, you were rolling the dice. In the end, even Ford got cold feet and – even though it stuck with the glue-in 'screens – it made sure the very next model got foam-filled A-pillars to give the roof even more crush strength.

Differential strokes

Plenty of new cars have early problems that cause a raft of component failures, even in their first weeks on sale. But when those failures start biting on the press launch, there are long faces all-round back at head office. That's what happened when Toyota pulled the covers off an all-new Corona back in the 1980s. Because it was a locally-sourced car, it used lots of locally-made parts to keep its Australian content high, including the rear differential (the Corona was Toyota's last mid-sized rear-drive car in this country).

The plan for the press launch was fairly simple: take a bunch of journos to the assembly plant, put them two-to-a-car in the new, fresh-off-the-production-line Corona, drive up into the NSW outback, stay at a pub overnight, get the journos full of steak and claret, and hey presto. Launch done. Except it didn't quite turn out that way.

By lunchtime on the first day, the first warning signs had been noted, Namely, that some of the journos could smell a gassy kind of odour. At the time, it was put down to a huge outback gas pipeline that shadowed the highway. Seemed plausible, too, but guess what? Nope, the smell was coming from Toyota differentials starting to cook themselves.

Pretty soon, one Corona succumbed to a rear diff that just kind of melted. The Toyota heavies shrugged and explained it away as a one-off. Until the second Corona also ground to a halt with the diff glowing bright red. Now brows were seriously furrowed. As

Driving a rear-drive Toyota Corona was not usually an exciting pursuit. Until the diff croaked in the middle of nowhere.

the launch continued, one by one, the Corona fleet started to have diff melt-downs until a large percentage had been abandoned for the tow truck to pick up later.

So what had gone wrong? It was kind of a simple mistake to make, really. The explanation (and this was according to Toyota at the time) was that a privately-bought Corona would be driven home from the showroom, then driven to work and back for a few weeks before being gently guided up the highway for annual holidays. What wouldn't happen to it, continued the official version, was that it would be plucked from the production line, filled with petrol and then driven at high speed over a long distance by a psychopathic car murderer disguised as a motoring journalist. The root problem, then, was that the differential never had time to 'run in' and learn to live happily beside its neighbouring components before being abused so horribly and completely. At which point it turned cherry-red, and then melted.

Frankly, there's probably something in this explanation, and back then it was not uncommon for press launch drives to become road-races as journos attempted to out-stupid each other. In the name of science and research, of course. And it would have been pretty easy for Toyota to blame the differential supplier for sending a batch of dud units, but it didn't, so full marks for taking it on the chin.

And the Corona itself? Um, 'dull' is a strong word, but it's fair to say that having a diff seize is probably the most exciting thing that ever happened to anybody driving a Corona of this vintage.

A painful history of the park brake

The park brake was perfected decades ago. You take a lever, mount it on the floor between the front seats, and run a cable to the actual brake on the wheels of the car. When you park the car, you pull up the lever and apply the brake. When you're ready to leave, you press the little button on the tip of the lever, lower it back to the floor, and away you go.

Nothing could be simpler, which is probably why car makers couldn't resist fiddling with it. Holden was a major cause of black thumbnails all over the country with a change to the park-brake arrangement on its VE Commodore model of 2006. The VE still used a handle mounted between the seats (in the centre console in a modern car) that you still pulled up to apply the brake, and lowered to release it. So far, so good.

The change was to move the release button from the tip of the lever to a button a few millimetres back from the tip, on the top face of the lever. The lever, when released, then dropped neatly into a slot in the centre console to become almost invisible (it actually then looked like a grab-handle, but anyway). However, the poor old end-user, conditioned by years and years of finding the release button at the tip of the lever, continued to attempt to do so. So while the tip of your thumb was trying to locate a button that wasn't there, the rest of your thumb triggered the actual button, prompting the lever

The Holden Commodore VE's park-brake lever; a thumb-squisher par excellence

to drop down into its slot. With your left thumb jammed between the lever and its hidey-hole. Ouch.

Bench seats caused a few headaches with hand-brake lever placement, with Holden's Kingswood and Chrysler's Valiant probably coming up with the best solution – a conventional floor-mounted lever that was simply mounted to the outside of the driver's side of the bench. It worked perfectly well and the only change required was that the lever needed to drop down out of the way when the brake was applied (to prevent snagging your Calvins as you slid across the seat to enter or leave the car). No biggie.

Ford's solution was to mount the lever as a pull-out job under the dashboard. You pulled the handle out to apply the brake, and turned the handle 90 degrees and let it slip back under the dash to release it. Not the ergonomic sweet spot that the floor-mounted type hit, but not too bad provided you could get enough muscle on it to apply the brake fully. Or actually reach the damn thing with your 1970s non-retractable seatbelt done up tight.

The real stinker was the style of park brake popular with American cars (and aped by some Euros and high-end Japanese cars) that used a foot pedal to apply the brake. To be honest, the ones that used a push on the pedal to apply the park brake and a second prod to release it weren't all bad. But the type that was applied the same way but used a separate knob on the dashboard to release it was just pants.

A mate of mine had a Holden Torana with just such an idiotic system. He was messing around with something under the dashboard with a torch in one hand and a screwdriver in the other, while lying on his back with his head in the footwell. Which was fine until his baby brother, ever helpful, grabbed the park-brake release handle and gave it a twist. The brake released, allowing the foot pedal to spring back to its normal position at about 100km/h. His rather voluminous head was squarely in the pedal's path. Yep: ouch again.

These days, the desire to shed weight has seen the emergence of the electronic park brake. And what a mess that's been. The idea that the car's computer can decide to release the brake if the car is in gear and attempting to move is fine (although the old-school red warning light and audible chime that you'd left the brake on didn't seem broken to me) but the electronics involved require more

The umbrella-handle park-brake was one solution ...

... as was this side-mounted job which still allowed for a bench front seat

These days, the desire to shed weight has seen the emergence of the electronic park brake. And what a mess that's been.

wiring and a motor to actually apply and release the brake. Lighter it might be, but less complex? Hardly. Beyond that, the electronic brake takes longer to apply or release, too, forcing you to sit for a moment while the motor does its thing. In the old days, you'd just drop the lever and be away. Even worse, some manufacturers thought it would be smart to have the electronic brake apply when the switch was pressed down, and release when it was pulled up. Which is exactly the opposite of what the familiar old lever did. Arrrggghh!

And there's one other major disadvantage with all this e-tech: the days of the hand-brake turn are now over. How a chap is supposed to impress a girl these days is anybody's guess.

It's raining – on the inside

Much has already been written about the styling disaster that was the AU Falcon of 1998 but, even beyond the visage that haunts Ford dealers to this day, the company's 'Edge' styling language imposed some practical problems as well. One of the most irritating was that the AU had virtually no drip rails. Throw in a roof that was significantly curved, and there was usually plenty of rainwater run-off.

This had a couple of knock-on effects. First, when you opened the door to get in after a rain shower, water often cascaded through the door opening. Some of it landed on the seat; most of it landed on you.

The second problem cropped up when it rained on a warm day (which in places like Queensland is the rule rather than the exception). Rather than crank up the air-con, it makes sense to open the driver's window a crack to get a bit of fresh air into the car. But again, the lack of a drip rail meant that water was free to stream into the car through that slightly open window. And when it did, it inevitably dropped on to the driver's armrest at the precise point where the horizontal power-window switches were located.

Water and electricity are never a good mix but, seriously, you could not have located this switch panel in a better spot for the rainwater to score a bullseye. Ford's stick-on weather shields for the front doors, needless to say, became a popular option with experienced AU owners.

WHICH SWITCH GOES WHERE?

It seems a bit odd to a frustrated designer like me that car companies don't standardise as much of a car's controls as they can. And yet, I still see cars with the indicator and windscreen-wiper stalks reversed, and a whole range of different solutions for gear-selectors and park-brake arrangements.

One of the real head-scratchers over the years is why some car makers place the power-window switches on the driver's armrest (or thereabouts) while others insist on mounting the switch panel in the centre console. You'd think the armrest would be the logical place, but there are actually a couple of really good reasons to mount the switches in the centre of the car.

They start with the fact that by mounting the switches centrally, you get to do away with the individual switches on either armrest. If either front-seat passenger can reach the central ones, why have a second one on the door? The central switch arrangement also reduces the amount of wiring inside the car and, these days, the wiring loom is a major contributing factor to the weight of a car, so that's good.

But the main reason for placing the switches in the centre of the car is all about simplifying the manufacturing differences when making the same car in both left- and right-hand drive. The switches in the middle remain the same for either left- or right-hand drive, while armrest-mounted switch panels (and the door trims themselves) need to be different, depending on which side of the car the driver sits.

Hot hatch's cold shoulder

When Peugeot's 205 GTi hot hatch hit the Australian market in 1987, it was a dead-set revelation and, in reality, our first taste of a real hot hatchback. We missed out on the original VW Golf GTi, so the 205 GTi was a real eyebrow-raiser in a country that, to that point, only understood a performance car as being a big, lumbering V8, and not a lightweight, nimble little hatch.

The 205's secret, of course, was classic hot-hatch stuff; cram a relatively big engine into a small hatchback, add alloy wheels, stir, and enjoy. It's a formula that's still in use today and it's fair to say that the hot hatch has gone on to represent the default formula for a performance car in the majority of countries around the world.

But, in the case of the 205 GTi, that concept created one big problem: the physically big 1.9-litre engine meant the 205's tiny engine bay was fuller than a Bathurst esky. And that meant that when Peugeot was specifying the car for Australia, it had an unenviable decision to make. Did it fit the car with air-conditioning OR power steering? Because fitting both was going to be impossible.

In the end, Peugeot took a look at Australia's average temperatures and opted for air-conditioning. Which was probably the right way to go. But you could always tell a 205 GTi owner by their huge biceps, a function of wrenching on that little steering wheel with no power assistance.

Peugeot's 206 GTi: you could have it with air-con or power steering, but not both!

Actually, Peugeot did eventually manage to engineer the car to retain the 1.9-litre engine as well as fit air-con AND power steering. But that didn't happen until 1991. Sure made for a nicer car, though.

GOING DIPPY

I mentioned a floor-mounted dipswitch to a colleague the other day and got a bucketful of blank looks. If you're too young to remember, the floor dipper was a little switch in the footwell that you stomped on to switch between high and low beam. Better than the current stalk stuff, too, because you didn't need to lift a single finger off the wheel. Progress, eh?

The direction-injection dilemma

The concept of direct fuel injection is a ripper. But let's start at the start: in conventional (old-school) fuel injection, the fuel and air are mixed at the intake port and then sucked into the engine (or blown in, in the case of a supercharged engine). But in a direct-injection engine (and they can be petrol or diesel) only the air passes through the ports and past the inlet valve, while the fuel is introduced directly into the combustion chamber.

And that's the direct-injection mantra: instead of injecting the fuel vapour from upstream of the inlet valve where it can fall out of suspension (become a liquid again) and then not burn as completely, why not inject it straight into the combustion chamber of the engine and have more control over the combustion process? Just for starters, you stand to pick up a 10 to 15 per cent gain in efficiency and performance. But, as it turns out, there are also a couple of why-not reasons.

The first of those revolves around the cleaning (or, in this case, non-cleaning) action of the fuel. By injecting the fuel straight into the combustion chamber, the fuel no longer washes the back of the inlet valve, cleaning it. This would be okay were it not for the fact that a modern engine also consumes a portion of its own exhaust gases (in the name of emissions control) as well as any crankcase fumes, which can include oil mist. And these re-enter the engine via – you guessed it – the inlet valves. Now all this gunk is collecting on the back of the inlet valve with no shot of fuel to clean it off. Over time, the carbon and other rubbish can clog the valve up to the point where it no longer seats properly and/or inhibits the flow of air into the engine. That's when you'll get the dreaded check-engine light and symptoms such as hard starting, a rough idle, poor fuel economy and reduced power.

Turbo-diesels with direct injection are even worse because that exhaust gas that gets recycled contains soot, which mixes with the oil fumes and forms a thick, black gunge. In either case, the end result needs to be removed or all those efficiency gains are down the toilet. Sometimes you'll get away with a specialty cleaning agent that is drawn into the engine as it runs, but, in a large number of cases, these deposits need to be tackled by disassembling the inlet side of the engine and cleaning the bits and pieces by hand. Fiddly, time consuming and expensive. But if you don't do it, as well as all those other problems, eventually a bit of this crap will break off, pass through the engine and lodge itself either in the turbocharger or the catalytic converter where it'll destroy those components, too.

The actual fuel injectors can also have a depressingly short life in a modern direct-injection diesel. Talk to mechanics and they'll tell you that hard-working modern turbo-diesels sometimes need new injectors well before the 100,000km mark. It varies from brand to brand, but these new injectors can cost anything up to $1000 (or more) per unit. Then there are the new filters and the labour that goes with it and, suddenly, that frugal turbo-diesel engine ain't looking so thrifty after all. In fact, early direct-injection diesel vehicles are now sometimes costing more for their big 150,000 or 200,000km service than the whole vehicle is worth, at which point you've got a real throwaway-society problem on your hands.

The other major catch with direct injection is that it needs to run at incredibly high pressures to work. In a conventional fuel-injected engine, the shot of fuel is sucked into the cylinder as the piston creates a vacuum as it moves down the cylinder. So all the injector really needs to do is atomise the fuel (turn it into a mist). Petrol doesn't mind this sort of treatment, so it doesn't require much pressure to achieve it.

But with direct-injection, you need to turn the fuel into a mist AND overcome the compression forces inside the cylinder, so the injector now has to atomise the fuel as well as shove it into a combustion chamber that's doing everything it can to spit its contents back out. So you need pressure, and lots of it. Typically, the numbers are in the thousands of psi and that requires electronic injectors, super-high-pressure pumps and even fuel rails that can withstand the force. So it's more expensive.

It's also dangerous; those are water-jet cutting pressures (you know, those machines that can slice through a block of steel using nothing more than water under high pressure). In fact, one of the big jobs for designers switching to direct injection was to make the fuel system tamper-proof. Because had Joe Average decided to have a fiddle with his car in the driveway on a Saturday morning and somehow managed to crack the fuel line with any residual pressure inside, he'd have lost the fingers on his spanner hand. No kidding!

Almost makes you want to go back to dirty, dribbly old carburettors. Nah.

The red D stands for direct injection: a double-edged sword if ever there was one

Because had Joe Average decided to have a fiddle with his car in the driveway on a Saturday morning and somehow managed to crack the fuel line with any residual pressure inside, he'd have lost the fingers on his spanner hand.

Double fault, FPV

Let's imagine you have developed a product to the point where its basic functions are well understood by the average working stiffs you're relying upon to buy the thing. You don't, for instance (or shouldn't), need printed instructions to know that taking the cap off the bottle is the best way to get the beer into your glass. Or that the hot tap is located to the left of the cold tap. Or that the curved bits of a pair of sunglasses go behind your ears, not in your eyes. And, thanks to decades of convention, we all know that starting a car requires you to place the key in the ignition switch and turn it clockwise. Er, yes. So why mess with it?

A few oddballs over the years, namely defunct Swedish funsters Saab, massaged the concept a little by placing the ignition switch in the space between the front seats. It was a safety thing: The key, safely tucked away between the chairs, would be much less likely to open an artery in your groin in the case of a decent shunt. Even then, it was still insert, twist the key to the right and Ikea here we come. Crucially, it was still a one-handed operation, leaving your other paw free to juggle your phone, take-away coffee, briefcase, house keys and, if you were the really dextrous type, to reach behind you and separate the kids who were already fighting. Yes, even in Sweden.

But was this level of user-friendliness good enough for Ford Australia's performance division, FPV, in the very early part of this century? Of course not.

A big, red starter button is racy and cool. Until you realise you need two hands to start the vehicle.

No, FPV decided that it had to offer its customers a more exotic, sportier experience. Simply starting the engine on these hotted-up taxis was not theatrical enough. Not by half. So, under a head honcho who'd spent time at Aston Martin in the UK, FPV borrowed that very James Bond-esque affectation, a starter button.

Now, a starter button is a good thing in a modern car with a proximity key that doesn't require you to even take that key out of your pocket. Using sensors, the car knows the key is within a certain range and will then unlock the doors and allow you to simply press a single button to fire the old girl up. But FPV, constrained by a limited budget, did only half the deal. See, you still had to use the key's remote to get into the car and you still had to insert that same key into the ignition barrel and turn it BEFORE you could press the starter button and have the engine burst into life.

That would have been a big enough J. Arthur Rank for most people, but it got worse: the ignition switch was in the usual place on the right-hand side of the steering column, but the 007-style starter button was to the left of the column, instantly turning the otherwise simple task of starting the engine into a two-handed test of coordination. As Q would have said: Pay attention, Bond!

The problem(s) with the rotary engine

I'll be up-front here and admit that I love rotary engines. So do a lot of people, but the finance departments of a few car companies definitely do not share my enthusiasm for the little 'chook cooker', as the rotary became known to some.

The rotary's most endearing properties are its apparent ability to rev like there's no tomorrow and to put out truly amazing gobs of horsepower, particularly if you turbocharge the thing. It's also smooth, since there are no pistons inside changing directions hundreds of times a second as there are in a conventional piston engine, threatening to tear the whole thing apart. The rotary is also a charismatic little guy and, while not everybody agrees with me, I reckon it sounds amazing, too.

Keeping everything spinning in the same direction is the secret to the engine's smoothness, and the key to its power output is the fact that the rotary makes power with every revolution, not every second revolution as with a four-stroke petrol engine.

But if the rotary is such a great piece of tech, what's it doing in this book? Well, charming and potent it may be, but early production versions of the rotary took a couple of fairly major manufacturers to the brink. One, Mazda, survived the rotary experiment, and the other, NSU, disappeared because of its early adoption of the concept.

Rotary engines were notorious for being unreliable. Yet it was a rotary that gave a Japanese maker its first win at Le Mans. So there.

The patent for the design of the rotary was taken out in 1929 by a German engineer, Felix Wankel. By spinning a vaguely triangular rotor inside a vaguely oval housing, Wankel was able to replicate the intake, compression, combustion and exhaust strokes of a piston engine, without the complexity of a camshaft and those incredible opposing forces inherent in an engine with pistons going up and down instead of round and round.

Plenty of companies looked at licensing the Wankel design, but most, after some test-bench failures, gave up on the idea and went back to piston-engine designs to power their products. All except two. NSU and Mazda both released rotary-powered cars in 1967 – the Ro80 and the Cosmo 110S respectively. But right away, the whole rotary experiment started to unravel.

The problems started out significant, and then got worse. For a start, the rotary likes to consume a bit of engine oil in the normal course of things. That was okay back in the 1960s when such behaviour was far from uncommon. Of greater concern was the engine's thirst. Sure, it made power like a 3.0-litre six-cylinder engine (even though it technically measured just on a litre) but it also drank like a big six. It was also a peaky little bugger, and needed to be revved hard to make that power (no real hardship given its appetite for revs). But the bigger problem was looming.

Fundamentally, the metallurgy of the day meant that the rotary engine's crucial apex seals (kind of the equivalent of a normal engine's piston rings) were failing, leading to a complete meltdown of the engine. Once the seals lost their efficiency, the engine would lose compression, become difficult to start and go further downhill until the engine failed altogether. At which point, you had a little pile of scrap metal under your bonnet.

Okay, so normal engines fail, too, but it was the short lifespan that was the rotary's undoing. And even before the engine was worn out, the rotary was prone to flooding and needed a careful warm-up procedure on the part of the driver. It's fair to say that had owners been a bit more switched-on, the failures might not have been so numerous or frequent. That said, it's hard to blame the buyers who were simply approaching their new Mazda as they had all their previous cars, yet were witnessing the thing self-destruct before its second oil change.

In many cases, that life expectancy was less than the meagre factory warranties offered in the day, and that was the root of the problem for both NSU and Mazda. In the case of the Ro80, many were fitted with multiple engines under warranty, but often with the same short-lived result. Eventually, the NSU company went out of business – partly because of the cost of replacing engines, but also because, after a while, word got out and nobody want to take a punt on an Ro80.

Mazda had a similar run of within-warranty failures with its early rotary-engined models, and, like NSU, it was financially wounded by the whole episode. Unlike NSU, though, Mazda was eventually bailed out by Ford which bought a big chunk of Mazda, thereby giving the Japanese brand the capital to regroup and fix the problems. If you've ever wondered why Mazda and Ford were model-sharing in the 1980s (the Ford Laser and Mazda 323, for instance) this bail-out is why.

Eventually, Mazda shifted its rotary attentions away from mainstream models and into sports cars, at which point the RX-7 franchise was born. Suddenly, the rotary was a viable thing and, as far as sports-car buyers were

Okay, so normal engines fail, too, but it was the short lifespan that was the rotary's undoing.

concerned, the previous reliability woes were less important than they would have been to a more conservative customer. Even so, many observers raised our eyebrows when, in the mid-1980s, Mazda turbocharged the rotary for the second-shape RX-7. In light of the engine's perceived frailties, this seemed incredible, but the blown rotary seemed to hang together, so Mazda got away with it.

Eventually, those hideous tailpipe emissions and thirst for unleaded caught up with the rotary such that, for the RX-8 of 2003, Mazda was forced to dump the turbocharger to clean up the engine's act. And with the turbo went a whole lot of performance and an even larger degree of personality. It's also worth noting that at least three motorcycle manufacturers – DKW, Suzuki and Norton – all had a crack at a rotary-powered production bike. But thanks to all the 'normal' problems, none of them really went the distance or remained in production very long at all.

But just to prove that the rotary could be made as reliable as it was powerful, back in 1991, a Mazda 787B sports car won the toughest motor race in the world, the Le Mans 24-Hour. Ironically, it wasn't outright pace (although with 520kW at 9000rpm it was hardly slow) but reliability that got the Mazda over the line, making it the first time a Japanese manufacturer had won the race. To put that into perspective, it took fellow Japanese giant Toyota another 27 years to match that feat.

Ford's Powershift failure

It's kind of unavoidable that car makers get stuff wrong. Cars are incredibly complex gadgets with lots and lots of moving, meshing parts. It doesn't take much to get even one of those little gizmos wrong and bring the whole shebang to a sorry halt by the side of the road. Were that not true, you wouldn't be reading this book.

But where it goes monumentally awry is when a manufacturer gets it all Pete Tong and then tries to blame the poor stiff who owned the thing when it went ker-bang. Which is what happened fairly recently with a range of cars Ford was selling around the world, including right here.

To be fair, the Ford Fiesta, Ecosport and Focus models equipped with the brand's six-speed clutchless manual transmission – dubbed PowerShift in Ford-speak – were otherwise quite decent cars. But the transmission itself was an unspeakable bastard of a thing. Failures started happening early in the cars' lifespan and by about 2015 the fan was buried under seven feet of you-know-what as owners suddenly found themselves with a transmission that either worked poorly, or didn't work at all.

Now, technical issues with clutchless manual gearboxes are definitely not confined to Ford. Volkswagen has also copped its share of flak over the same technology, and the problems are largely similar – clutch packs dying early, and underdone bits of the

Double-clutch gearboxes are just trouble. Ford's was the poster-child for mechanical mayhem.

transmission wearing out and dumping metallic particles into the transmission fluid, which are then attracted to the magnetic sensors that control the whole show. With predictable results. It's also worth mentioning that versions of this type of gearbox with wet clutch packs (that run in fluid) are nowhere near as bad as the lighter, cheaper versions that use dry clutch packs; but it's no exaggeration to suggest that a lot of car buyers have sworn off clutchless manuals forever.

Volkswagen (and others) have at least had the sense to cop the failures on the chin and try to keep their customers happy by introducing a raft of running changes and software updates to minimise the woes. Not Ford Australia. Nope, Ford decided to blame the end user for the tranny failures, suggesting that even though the car was marketed and sold just like any other two-pedal (automatic) car, you lot out there are driving them wrong. You can't, for instance, said Ford Oz, hold the car on a hill with just the gearbox stopping it slipping back. Which makes sense if you're a transmission engineer, but of no use whatsoever to the person who bought a Ford hatchback thinking it was just like any other automatic.

And you can bet the brochure never mentioned anything about this stuff.

Finally, in the face of massive consumer backlash, Ford Australia started offering owners of the affected cars a trade-up deal to the newer model. Crucially, it had a conventional automatic transmission, Ford having dumped the whole clutchless manual concept in the nearest skip (its only half-smart move in this whole sorry mess). Which is about when the country's highest consumer advocacy body, the Australian Competition and Consumer Commission (ACCC), started wagging its finger in Ford's direction.

You know you're in the ka-ka when the most powerful consumer protection body in the land takes you on and accuses you in the Federal Court of 'unconscionable conduct'. And you can be even more certain you're in it up to your corporate neck when the court agrees and orders you to pay 10 million bucks in penalties.

It all boiled down to Ford's initial refusal to take responsibility for selling thousands of people a pup. The Federal Court ruling took into account Ford's efforts to deal with the problem and concluded it should have done more. Ford was harshly criticised for failing to replace or refund the cost of faulty cars, even though some owners had experienced multiple replacement transmissions that would simply break, just like the last one(s).

Eventually, Ford Oz fell on its sword (although not until the court ruling was announced) with president and CEO, Graeme Whickman, admitting: '... we took too long to identify the issues and we acknowledge that PowerShift customers did not have complaints handled appropriately between May 2015 and February 2016.

'We were overwhelmed with the volume of complaints and, while it was not intended, over a 10-month period our processes were inadequate and information provided was either inaccurate or incomplete. We let our customers down and for that we are sorry.'

Finally, Whickman hit the nail on the head: 'Of particular concern was the Owner Loyalty Program, which resulted in customers paying an additional cost to buy new vehicles although they may have been eligible for a refund or no-cost replacement vehicle. We now realise this program was flawed as it didn't ensure an

... the smart money says closer to half of all the affected cars have been fixed at least once as a result of this horrible, dodgy little gearbox.

adequate assessment of customers' rights under consumer law.'

Just to put a fork in all of this, about 75,000 cars were thought to be affected in Australia alone, and while Ford admits that something like 10,500 individual customer cases have been opened, the smart money says closer to half of all the affected cars have been fixed at least once as a result of this horrible, dodgy little gearbox.

As far as the Federal Court and the ACCC are concerned, many of those owners should have been given replacement cars or had the opportunity to give their cars back to Ford and receive a full refund. Ford offering to take more money from them to upgrade to a newer car was just not good enough. And as for blaming the cars' owners for what was a design flaw in the first place, well, that's the really thin end of the wedge.

And will it happen again? Maybe not to Ford Australia and maybe not as a result of a crap transmission. But yep, our money would be on things continuing to go wrong and some car makers being advised against doing the right thing.

Swept up in a design urge

Have you noticed the trend towards upswept waistlines in newer cars? Jump from an old-school car with its big window areas into something modern like a small SUV, and chances are you'll come over all claustrophobic, particularly in the back seat where the window line rises sharply, leaving you looking at upholstery rather than the scenery.

My own theory on this is that car makers have gone down this stylistic road on the basis of trying to make unsporty shapes look a little more sporty. The problem begins when you attempt to make a small car with a small footprint into an SUV. To make sure the car can actually accommodate enough people and their luggage, the compact floor area dictates that the cabin itself has to be a bit upright. Sure, you can round off the edges, but then it just looks like a dumpling with headlights.

The other way to make it look less gumby is to sweep up the waistline and attempt to give the impression that the car has some kind of fastback thing going on. As in: if you can't slope the roof down, then visually sweep the rest of the rear-end up. I don't think it works, but then I don't think like your typical SUV buyer, either.

Anyway, the upshot is that you have a steeply rising window-line in the rear seat which, typically, is where the kids are doomed to sit. In a lot of cases, the window-line is above the eyeline of said youngsters. As anyone with kids will immediately point out, nothing makes a rug-rat burp its breakfast faster than not being able to see out of a moving vehicle.

The other trick car makers are playing right now as part of the same subterfuge is to hide the rear door handles as a means of making the car look like a two-door (that faux fastback thing again). Only catch there is that the actual door handle is often 'hidden' in the window surround which, thanks to that damn upswept window-line, is already way up off the ground. And if you've ever seen three-year-old Little Miss Independent demand to open her door herself despite being unable to reach the handle, you'll know that's never going to play well.

COLOUR SECRETS

Ever noticed that the colour palette of 1970s Volvos and Volkswagen Beetles is similar? Actually, not similar, they're identical. But why?

It's simple: both the Volvo 240 and the Beetle were assembled in Melbourne at what became the Nissan plant at Clayton, in the city's south-east. And while they went down separate assembly lines within the same factory, they were both painted in the same paint shop.

Management decided that rather than change the colours for each make, they'd simply paint Volvos and Beetles the same range of colours. Oh sure, they gave the colours different names – what VW called Flipper Blue was known at Volvo as Light Blue – but take it from us, they were the same colours applied by the same spray-guns in the same paint shop.

Poor gear selection

If there's a modern technology that has 'blind alley' written all over it, it would have to be the clutchless manual transmission. The idea is fine: make a gearbox that is as simple to use as an automatic, but with the fuel efficiency of a manual. The reality, however, has been rather different.

Oh sure, the clutchless manual (or DSG, DCT, SMG or PDK; pretty much every manufacturer has their own acronym for the same technology) does offer two-pedal operation and it can be more fuel efficient than a conventional automatic. Hell, it can even make shifts so fast that neither an automatic nor a conventional human-operated manual can hope to match it. And, yes, they can be lightweight, and even quite nice to use. But they can also be super-dodgy fragile.

The whole concept was the result of motorsport engineers looking for a way to shift gears faster than a driver ever could. By allowing a computer to control the clutch (or clutches – a lot of newer designs have twin-clutch packs) and select each gear, the robotised manual (yet another name for them) can slot gears in fractions of a second. The problem with that, of course, is that race cars only have to race one race at a time; meanwhile, your family wheels is expected to work properly for hundreds of thousands of kilometres and many, many years. Nor is smoothness and refinement of particular concern to the average race car engineer or designer.

Early clutchless manuals were almost literally a manual gearbox with a computer controller for the clutch, and selectors bolted on. In a race car, the harsh, stilted shifts didn't matter, but in a road car they were god-awful with lots of shunting and snatching and banging noises coming from under the car. That led designers to come up with an improved version called the twin-clutch that, as the name suggests, uses a pair of clutch packs and basically divides the gearbox into two. This was a much smoother, more refined transmission, but came with its own baggage. Even then, they weren't always super smooth and cars such as the Nissan GT-R that use a twin-clutch design are still pretty awful in stop-start traffic.

Meantime, even if the twin-clutch is generally more refined, the sheer level of complexity involved – aside from making them expensive (especially to replace) – also means there's lots that can go wrong. And boy, does it. Actually, let me qualify that: Porsche seems able to make a durable one (called a PDK) but it seems like everyone else has experienced long-term durability dramas with the concept. Ford has been hauled over the coals by the ACCC for its crappy Powershift versions, and plenty of Volkswagen owners have also experienced the DSG blues.

The major problem seems to be the clutch packs, which can wear out early, but various other problems, including shot bearings and sensors that stop sensing, have been catalogued. When they're working properly, they can be decent fun, especially with a set of paddle shifters to control them. Until they go bang. And then they're no fun at all.

The reality, too, is that the conventional automatic gearbox with a lock-up torque converter has kind of caught up with the clutchless manual in terms of shift speed, lightness and number of gears. As a result, we're already seeing some manufacturers step away from the clutchless manual while those who never took the plunge are thanking their lucky stars. It's often said that the conventional manual with a clutch pedal is an endangered species (on the grounds of tailpipe emissions); but it wouldn't surprise anyone if its robotised cousin is the first one to be blindfolded and stood against the wall.

Ranger danger lurks at service time

It might be bolted together in Thailand, but the Ford Ranger ute and its Mazda BT-50 badge-brother are actually Australian designs. All the concept, design and engineering work was done by Ford Oz as part of Ford's design and manufacturing globalisation. Which, if you wanted to be cynical, is another way of saying that, while Ford doesn't make cars here any more, head office was good enough to throw us a bone with the contract to design the Ranger.

Regardless of where it's made, the Ranger has gone on to become a huge seller for Ford Down Under. In fact, for the last couple of years, it has been the brand's biggest-selling model and perhaps even Ford Oz's genuine saviour. However, that doesn't mean the Ranger doesn't come complete with a trap for young players. Or old ones, for that matter. It's not a flaw per se, but there is one thing you need to be aware of before picking up the spanners.

The potential trap surfaces when the Ranger is due for a service. Not that it's any more complex a piece of machinery than any other turbo-diesel ute, but there is one tiny, teensy bit of information you have to have, or your first Ranger service could be your last. And that starts when, as part of any normal servicing, you go to change the oil.

The trick is that the Ranger's engine uses a chain-driven oil pump. That

The first instinct of many people, on seeing that the oil pressure light is still glowing, is to give the engine a rev. Bad move.

doesn't sound too startling, but the pump's design decrees that if it isn't sitting in oil, it will bleed dry and then refuse to prime itself once the engine restarts. And if that happens, the engine is suddenly running without oil pressure which, as any mechanic will tell you, is a fast lane to shrapnel.

This would be less than a problem if it wasn't for the way busy commercial workshops work. Often a car will have its sump plug removed and then the mechanic will move on to the next task (or morning tea) while the oil drains completely. Then he or she will return half an hour (or several hours later) to change the oil filter, replace the sump plug, fill the engine with fresh oil and then hit the key while the front office writes out the customer's invoice.

But try that with a Ranger, and you'll soon find that leaving the sump plug out for any more than about 10 minutes will result in the oil pump pulling that bleeding-dry stunt. And the first the mechanic will know about it will be when they start the car and the oil pressure warning light on the dashboard doesn't go out. Which is when part two of the problem occurs. The first instinct of many people, on seeing that the oil pressure light is still glowing, is to give the engine a rev. Bad move.

None of this was so much of a problem when Rangers were new and still being serviced by Ford dealerships under warranty. But as they aged, changed hands and mechanics without Ford's factory training stepped in, oil pressure lights were glowing all over the place. The fix to reprime the oil pump is anything but a simple one, too, and that's provided you HAVEN'T blown the engine up in the process.

Turning up the heat on diesel cars

Engineers and car owners got themselves painted into a bit of a corner in the early part of this century, thanks to a combination of tightening emissions controls and a lack of understanding among owners. And it was all to do with the nouveau sexiness of owning a diesel passenger car.

The cult of the diesel meant that more and more people were driving oil-burners than ever before, while ever-tougher pollution controls were demanding fewer tailpipe emissions from those same diesel cars. The solution for many car makers was a thing called the Diesel Particulate Filter (DPF), or soot filter to you and me.

The broad idea was that the filter would collect anything up to 80 per cent of the black smoke produced by a diesel engine, and – literally – trap it inside the filter. Of course, it couldn't do that forever, so when the filter became full of soot, it would regenerate itself. Now, regeneration in this sense is an interesting choice of words, because what basically happens is that the on-board computer heats the soot filter up to a temperature of about 600 degrees and burns it clean.

To a simpleton like me, this sounds awfully like picking up after your dog and then dumping those same dog's eggs on a nature strip one street away. Surely, storing soot and then burning it off somewhere else is moving the pollution rather than actually preventing it. Of course, the emissions legislation in question demands a limit to the soot that is introduced into the atmosphere for the duration of the official laboratory test procedure. It says nothing about what happens to it when you get one street away. So the soot filter was a cheap way of adhering to the letter of that somewhat odd law.

And it worked, too. Mostly. Well, it did while ever the car was being driven as a diesel should be. That is, it got used for a decent run down a highway or freeway at least once a month or so. The problem was, however, that Australian car buyers, so enamoured with the lazy flexibility and fuel economy of the latest generation of turbo-diesels, were buying them but driving them exactly the same way as they used their previous petrol-powered cars. Which is to say, they'd start them, drive three minutes to the shops/school/work in stop-start, low-speed traffic, and then shut them down until it was time to go three minutes the other way back home.

Now, to understand the problem with that, you need to look at the design of the DPF and how it regenerates itself. The idea was that once the soot filter started to get full, the computer would wait until the next run down a freeway - at which point the exhaust system was hot enough - and then instruct the filter to burn itself off. Trouble was, for a lot of these first-time diesel owners, the exhaust was never getting that hot, thanks to all the short-run use.

Never fear, said the engineers, we'll make sure the exhaust gets hot enough regardless of the owner's driving habits, and we'll do that by tipping extra fuel into the engine on the exhaust stroke. This will heat up the exhaust system and allow the regeneration to occur. Which it often did. But there was a sometimes fatal flaw in that logic.

While the majority of the fuel did, indeed, go to heating up the exhaust system, in some cases, some of it wound up getting past the piston rings and into the sump where it mixed with - and, crucially, diluted - the engine's lubricating oil. At that point, you had a sump full of oil that was no longer capable of completely and properly protecting the engine from friction and, bingo, you had accelerated engine wear. Complete engine failures were not unknown.

And because all this was happening beneath the surface (the driver had no say in it) the first time some people knew anything was up was when they dipped their oil and discovered that the level in the sump had actually increased. Even this only rang an alarm bell if the owner could remember how much was in the sump last time they checked, and - even more critically - provided they even bothered to check the dipstick at all on their brand-new vehicle.

The problem first came to our notice in diesel versions of the Mazda CX-5 SUV, which used Mazda's SkyActiv technology that made do with a much lower compression ratio than most diesels (which may or may not have had something to do with Mazda being the first to start having problems). But before too long, other makes and models had started to run afoul of the same problem. Even then, it was a while before someone worked out what was happening, but once they did, the soot filter and its requirement to be periodically purged was fingered as the culprit.

Mazda's solution was to revise the computer's program to change the way it handled that extra fuel, to avoid it gurgling down into the sump. Oh, and issuing owners with a revised dipstick with a new upper mark on it.

So why not just go for a decent drive every few weeks to keep the soot filter happy? Well, that would work, but if a car locks you into driving somewhere you don't need to go each month, aren't you kind of tearing up a large part of the appeal (lower running costs) of a turbo-diesel engine?

Eventually, too, we started to realise that even though a diesel engine could stretch a litre of fuel further, there were other concerns. They started with the emissions being a particularly nasty combination of carcinogenic oxides of nitrogen, extended to more frequent (and therefore costlier) maintenance, and finished with always having a slimy, grimy hand and stinky shoes after filling up (diesel doesn't evaporate, so it sticks to the fuel nozzle and pools on the ground where you stand to fill the car. By the third time you fill up, your carpets will also smell of diesel).

Within a decade or so, diesel had fallen off the sexy radar and we went

To a simpleton like me, this sounds awfully like picking up after your dog and then dumping those same dog's eggs on a nature strip one street away.

back to buying small and medium passenger cars with conventional petrol engines and even hybrid drivelines that could kick a diesel's backside for urban-cycle fuel economy. Petrol engines had also, by then, seriously closed the gap to the diesels in fuel economy terms and were much, much nicer to drive and live with. And they kept your boots clean.

The heavy transport industry will stick with diesel, mainly because fuel economy is so critical and also because hybrids lose their efficiency advantage on longer journeys. And you know what? That's maybe where diesel should stay.

The politics of stupid

DUMB LAWS AND CORPORATE DECISIONS

As unhappy as Larry

In an age when company CEOs at the big end of town are often rewarded for a lousy corporate performance with huge bonuses and share packages, it's tempting to think we might have been a little less generous of spirit back in the old days. Certainly, that's the conclusion you have to draw when you look at what happened to a bloke by the name of Sir Laurence (call me Larry) Hartnett.

Hartnett was a Brit who was appointed as managing director of General Motors Holden in 1934. A born salesman and what we'd now call an ideas man, Hartnett took his role very seriously and embraced his new country and company with enthusiasm. He was something of a war hero during World War II, flying to Europe several times in stunningly dangerous circumstances to help out with the Australian war effort of which Holden was a big manufacturing part.

After the war, he got serious about the question of what to do with Holden's production capacity and what many saw as a pressing need to get Australia on its own wheels. A succession of Australian prime ministers discussed this question with General Motors management, but it was Hartnett who got the I's dotted and T's crossed.

Yet despite him being central to Australia ever making a single car, he was then demonised and effectively warehoused by his own company just

Australia would possibly never have built cars without Larry Hartnett. Yet Holden unceremoniously unfriended him just as the industry got its act together.

two years before the first Holden was launched on 29 November, 1948. By then, the Holden car had been being developed and fine-tuned for many years, but Hartnett was probably most responsible for it happening at all. As it was, though, he was not involved in the final product-planning decisions.

At the time, General Motors recalled Hartnett to head office in New York, believing he'd become too Australianised and too headstrong. Hartnett refused to return, however, and elected to resign and stay in Australia, where he and his family had been living for more than a decade.

The real slap in the face came as Hartnett was left off the invitation list for the famous unveiling of Australia's Own Car in late 1948. The images of a smiling Prime Minister Ben Chifley standing next to the first Holden 48/215 are familiar to all, but you won't find Larry Hartnett's face in any of them. Even if you subscribe to the view that Hartnett could be a bit abrasive and that he was perhaps on pretty good terms with himself, it still seems like a terrible insult to one of the true pioneers of our local car industry.

Snowstorm in Melbourne? Ford will be ready

Once the decision was taken by Ford in the late 1950s to start production of the Falcon here in Australia, it was painfully obvious that the existing Geelong plant couldn't cope. It was too small, for starters, and not designed to house almost 3000 workers cranking out 200 cars per day. So Ford did a deal with the Victorian government and got a specially rezoned, bargain-priced 180-hectare chunk of flat, featureless land north of Melbourne and built its new production plant and head office in Broadmeadows.

But here's where it gets silly: the roof of the four-storey head office building is designed to cope with the weight of eight feet of snow. Since the only meteorological activity of any note in Broadmeadows is the prevailing south-west wind and sometimes a blast-furnace northerly in summer, that seems a bit odd. Yet to Ford management back in 1958, when the building was announced, it was entirely logical. It all stems from the fact that Ford's blueprints for anything called a head office were designed with the US generally, and Detroit specifically, in mind. That's where the eight-feet-of-snow thing makes sense, in its own strange way.

When you think about it now, the idea of Australia's head office being built according to company practice – regardless of the fact that it was fundamentally inappropriate – is a perfect metaphor for Ford today, and all the other companies that used to build cars here. The pursuit of a

Plonked in outer Melbourne, Ford's head office stands as a monument to global misunderstanding

universally acceptable car concept has meant that cars are now designed as global models, with no regard for specific market requirements. Which, to some extent, is how we lost the Falcon and all the other Aussie-made cars. And how we ended up with a four-storey snow-shelter in a dry paddock in Broadmeadows.

What if Ford Australia had said to Detroit, 'hang on, we don't need a roof that'll cop eight feet of frozen rain; we can get away with something lighter and cheaper'? Surely, the cost of re-engineering the roof for local conditions would have been cheaper than the sheer cost of materials and over-engineering for a snow-proof roof. Probably, but I guess we'll never know.

SCREWED OVER

If you've ever had a Phillips-head screw become distorted and mangled because you used the wrong-sized screwdriver, you probably hate the things. And you may well question the wisdom of their invention in the first place. I mean, why not use the old faithful slotted-head screw that was a lot harder to mangle? Well, you can thank factory automation. The Phillips-head screw came about in the 1930s as global industry was moving towards the production-line concept and automated assembly in a big way. The self-centring nature of the Phillips-head design meant it was perfect for production lines where powered, automated screwdrivers were used. One of the first adopters was GM, which used Phillips-head screws on the production line of its 1936 Cadillac.

Ford dumps the V8

Of all the nutty, loopy decisions made over the years by the management of Australian car companies, the one that must surely rate right up there with the most inexplicable is Ford's decision to drop the V8 engine option from its popular Falcon line-up.

Despite being the company that made a V8 engine in a mainstream model a reality in this country; despite the V8 giving the whole Falcon range a performance halo; despite in-house research showing that more than half of Falcons were ordered with towbars; despite the cries of horror from the Falcon faithful; despite the unquestionable improvement to the driving experience the V8 provided; despite the prospect of handing the performance family-car market to Holden; despite everything: Ford decided that for the 1983 model year, Aussie buyers weren't getting a V8 Falcon.

What was just as loony about the decision was that the XE was the first Falcon to have overtaken its Holden opposite number in the sales race. By keeping the V8 on tap, Ford could have potentially stretched that trend even further. But, possibly through corporate arrogance and its faith in the fleet market (which cared not for V8 engines), it didn't. Ford must have imagined that it could hold Holden at bay even without the V8 option; and while the XF did sell well, a V8 option for the Falcon could have buried Holden even deeper. Opportunity lost.

A V8 engine in a four-door sedan has long been the sweet spot for Aussie family cars. So what was Ford thinking back in 1983?

The results for Ford (and even back then it must have been obvious what was going to happen) were predictable. Those for whom the V8 grunt and soundtrack were a part of life switched camps to Holden. Oh, it wasn't as simple as that; the Holden Commodore was a physically smaller car than the XF Falcon, so there was a price to pay. But, ultimately, Ford handed thousands of car buyers to Holden on a silver flamin' tray. Holden never looked back. And Ford never really recovered.

In fact, there are those within the industry to this day who point to 1983 and the axing of the V8 Falcon as some kind of first step in the demise of Ford as a maker of cars in this country. And you know what? They're probably right.

The other part of the problem was Ford's alternative to the mighty V8. The idea was that a new, electronically fuel-injected version of the Falcon's six-cylinder engine would provide the replacement for the bent-eight. And, sure, it was a better mousetrap than the carburetted six, but it was sure as hell no V8. And the punters damn well knew it. Ford's next move was to make the six-cylinder (semi-) modern with an overhead camshaft and more performance. But even then, after about a decade of denying its customers the V8 option, it changed its mind, importing a batch of injected 5.0-litre V8s and reinstating the V8 box on the order form. It was, of course, far too late to save the brand's bacon as a maker of performance family cars.

So why do it? Why, in the heyday of the V8 engine in this country, would you simply pull the pin on it? Nobody who wasn't in the boardroom that day will ever know for sure, but it's a fair bet that Ford saw itself as a volume car maker that didn't need to mess about with niche models like V8 family cars. And, naturally, it was wrong. The other topic of concern was an anticipated fuel crisis and rising per-litre prices at the pump. But as history has shown, there's a percentage of Aussie car buyers who will pay the extra petro-bucks each week for the pleasure of driving a V8.

Not that Holden is entirely without sin. Back in 1984, there were rumours that Holden, too, would dump its locally-made V8 in the face of rising fuel prices. Holden was probably equally worried about the cost of developing the old V8 into something that could live with unleaded petrol, which was mandated for all new cars from 1 January, 1986; even in '84, that edict had Holden chasing its engineering tail. So when Holden's boss at the time, Chuck Chapman, evaded answering questions at a 1984 press conference over the future of the Holden V8, the journos started an uprising.

The 'V8s 'till 98' campaign was born and, with help from various magazines aimed at the V8-lovin' car buyer, Holden was convinced to change its mind and spend up big on making the local V8 work on unleaded. And luckily it did, because once the folly of Ford's decision had really hit home, it was clear to Blind Freddy that there were enough Aussies who wanted V8s that it would have been marketing suicide to walk away. As Ford was just starting to find out. The hard way.

The car that started the whole V8 thing for many Australians; the XR Falcon GT

Sharing, not caring

Model sharing, also known as badge-engineering, is where a car maker plonks its own badge on a car from another maker in a – typically unsuccessful – attempt to get a foot in the door of a market segment in which it wasn't previously active.

The reasons for two car companies ganging up and entering a model-sharing deal are many and varied; but in Australia in the mid-1980s, it was all about survival of the car industry. The Button Plan (the brain-child of Senator John Button, working within the Hawke federal government) aimed to get locally-made cars up to production volumes that made them financially viable. As a way of saving the industry, it was a rather clever concept. As it panned out once the car companies had interpreted the idea? Um, less so.

The forced marriages that were part of the Button Plan produced some very strange fruit indeed, including a Nissan Patrol bearing Ford Maverick badges, a Nissan Pulsar that became a Holden Astra, and a Toyota Corolla rebadged as a Holden Nova – memorable for being Holden's most reliable model ever, despite not a-c-t-u-a-l-l-y being made by Holden. Predictably, the Australian car buyer was not seduced by these developments and the badge-engineered versions of each car flopped, usually in spectacular fashion.

But there's one product of the Button Plan that deserves special mention for a level of odious cynicism that

How can a re-badged Commodore be a tribute to a bloke famous for his creativity and original thinking?

even (some) politicians might have baulked at. But not Toyota. See, as part of the deal to provide Holden with Novas (Corollas) and Apollos (Camrys), Holden's end of the bargain was to provide Toyota with VN Commodores that were badged, without a hint of irony, as the Toyota Lexcen.

If you're too young to remember, Ben Lexcen was the gifted designer of the racing yacht *Australia II*, the winged-keel wonder that finally relieved the US of the America's Cup in 1983. Lexcen, who died at just 52 years of age in 1988, was not only a great designer, he was a brilliant lateral thinker, innovator and creator of original ideas and concepts. All of which makes Toyota's decision to put his name to a fairly ordinary, six-cylinder family car that wasn't even Toyota's own work, seem more like an insult than a pat on the back. Or a nasty cash-in at best.

Cheating on the test

Back in 1988 when Ford's all-new EA Falcon was released, a huge part of the hype was about the new overhead-camshaft six-cylinder engine. Forget that Europe had been building overhead cam engines that had powered everything from Noah's Ark to the Ferris wheel at the Colosseum. Putting one in an Aussie Falcon was still big news.

Aside from the improved performance and smoothness the new engine offered, one of its big selling points was fuel efficiency. I was working for a mainstream car magazine at the time, and when we sat down and looked at a map, it seemed possible – if a little sketchy – that this new Falcon could conceivably get from Melbourne to Sydney on a single tank of unleaded: an unheard-of prospect until then.

Crunching the numbers, it seemed like a chance. We chose the lightest version of the new Falcon, with the most economical of the new engines, and specified the more frugal manual transmission variant. Based on Sydney's CBD post office being 878km away from Melbourne's, and using the official highway fuel consumption figure for the car of 7.6 litres per 100km, the calculator spat out a figure of 66.728, which was the number of litres we'd need. The Falcon's fuel tank held 68 litres. So it would be close, but either way, it'd be a good read. (Besides which, the journo who volunteered to do the drive conveniently needed to be in Sydney for a wedding that weekend.)

Late on a Friday night, the car was driven gently away from the Melbourne post office (no traffic at that hour to hold things up) and the great economy drive was on. By keeping his speed down to around 80 or 90km/h, the journo was able to keep the Falcon in its economy sweet spot; although staying awake as the white posts ambled by was, apparently, the greater challenge.

Finally, the next day and with the orange fuel-level warning light glowing since about Bowral, the Falcon idled smoothly to a stop in front of the Sydney GPO. Mission accomplished. It was all smiles until the journo went to fill the car to head to the wedding. Somehow, even though we were dealing with a 68-litre tank, the EA managed to swallow just on 72 litres. Wait a minute ...

At first Ford tried stonewalling. But, faced with the realisation that we were going to call them out whatever happened, they came clean, admitting that they'd loosened the straps that hold the plastic fuel-tank in the EA Falcon. This allowed the tank to droop and bulge a bit, giving it those extra few – and probably all-important – litres. So you cheated then? Not exactly, claimed Ford. See, we've found that, over the years, the straps tend to stretch and sag a little on their own, so really, we were only hurrying up that process!

LPG TO THE RESCUE

A nice side-effect of running on LPG is that it's much harder to cook an engine by overheating it. LPG will freeze in the mixer as it depressurises, so the mixer itself is hooked into the engine's cooling system. Essentially, the coolant that keeps the engine cool also keeps the mixer warm and the LPG flowing. Logically, then, if the car loses coolant, the mixer runs dry and the gas freezes, stopping the car in its tracks before the lack of coolant can do major harm to the engine. Nice. One more reason to go gas.

New car smell, or scent of burning money?

Remember that scene from Stephen King's *Christine* where the hapless Arnie buys a pile-o-crap Plymouth from the crusty brother of the original owner? And remember how the old guy was describing that new-car smell? Okay, there was a certain human-pheromone reference I won't go into here, but the point was that a brand new car is something absolutely special.

And it is. But buying a brand-spanker is also one of the sketchiest financial investments you can make. From the moment you leave the dealership, the little numerals counting the car's current value are winding backwards at a horrendous rate. In a lot of cases, give it three years and the car will be worth roughly half its original value. That's when people make the other great mistake: They trade-in on the next new money pit.

A pragmatic buyer waits until the car is three years old and then buys a really nice, clean second-hand one, usually the upmarket version with all the convenience and safety equipment because it won't be much dearer than the poverty-pack model. And these days, when cars have never been better built or more reliable, a three-year-old car is not an old clunker by any means. Even better, the original owner will have dealt with any teething problems and attended to any recalls. And, of course, taken that big financial hit for you.

Seriously, with a few exceptions, buying brand new cars is a mug's game. And here's another tip: if you must have that elusive new car smell, you can actually buy a scent that replicates the whiff of a dealership-fresh interior. Second-hand car dealers use it all the time!

Don't be fooled by the new-car smell. It won't last.

NO MAN IS AN ISLAND

From the You Can't Make This Stuff Up department: the first traffic islands in the world were built in Liverpool, England in 1862, but the most ill-fated was the first built in London, in St James Street in 1864. It was privately commissioned by one Colonel Pierpoint, who was concerned that he was going to be run down by a horse and carriage on his way to (but more likely home from) his private club in Pall Mall. After much work and money, his traffic island was finished and the good colonel rushed across the street to inspect it. And was mown down and killed by a horse and carriage. True story.

HSV Group A SS – too much of a good thing

Even when it looks like you're on a winner, you can sometimes get too greedy. Back in 1988, the newly-formed Holden Special Vehicles (established after Holden divorced Peter Brock) was ready to whip the covers off its first headline product, the Group A SS.

Not only was this car set to be the flagship model in HSV showrooms, it also formed the basis of the cars that would carry Holden's hopes in touring car racing both in Australia and overseas (Group A racing was a global formula). Homologation cars like the Group A SS have always struck a chord with Aussie petrol-heads, so it was no surprise that the first 500 Group As were snapped up by keen punters who recognised a slice of motorsport history when they saw it.

Now, you can make up your own mind about the car itself; but it's fair to say that the wild collection of plastic add-on panels (all aimed at improving the aerodynamics and, therefore, speed of the racing version) gave it … let's just call it a 'distinctive' look. Within a short space of time, the car had earned the rather unkind moniker of 'the plastic pig'.

The problems started for HSV when it got a bit greedy and decided to make an extra 250 of the things to satisfy customer demand (and bulk out its bank account; the car cost $45,000 when a Holden V8 Calais was about 14 grand cheaper). Only problem was,

Plastic Pig, Batmobile; call it whatever nasty names you like, but I bet you wish you had one now

not only did the initial run of 500 satisfy the homologation rules, but also consumer demand. So those last couple of hundred Group As sat around in dealerships like stale bottles of beer.

In the end, dealers were removing body kits from unsold cars and offering them up as 'normal' Holdens in an attempt to shift them off the lot. It didn't help that it took until 1990 for the Group A SS to finally win the annual Bathurst 1000 – well after it was even available to buy. But the win did cement the car's place in local motorsport history and virtually guaranteed its collectibility. That's how it sometimes goes in the collector-car world, and a Group A SS these days is still a striking-looking car, but you'll need deep pockets to get behind the wheel. Ironic, when they couldn't give 'em away back in the day.

Just the fax, ma'am

These days, the idea of a car being connected with the outside world is anything but extraordinary. In fact, a brand-new car without sat-nav, Apple CarPlay and Android Auto connectivity is the exception rather than the rule; but there was a time when bringing the rest of the world into your car was decidedly extravagant. And sometimes, time can be so cruel ...

I picked up a HSV SV88 test car back in the day (1988, not too surprisingly) from the brand's head office in Melbourne's south-east. Normally, you'd grab the keys from reception, match the registration number on the keyring with a car in the carpark (not everything had remote central locking back then), jump in and make sure there was a press kit in a folder on the passenger's seat.

The first two of these steps went well with this particular SV88 (a V8 Commodore with a subtle body kit and some other executive express-oriented changes) but the press kit that should have been on the seat was nowhere to be seen. In its place, however, was a plastic box about the size of a ream of paper with some leads hanging out of it, disappearing under the seat.

Before I could go back inside to ask, HSV's boss, the towering John Crennan, leaned in through the passenger's window and said enigmatically: 'I'll fax you the press kit on the move'. Yep, the box beside me was a fax machine. At the time,

The gadget on the passenger's seat is indeed a portable fax machine. Yuppies were wetting their pants in 1988.

this was a real wow of an idea but, like I said, time can be cruel and the whole thing looks pretty strange now. Especially since fax machines were all done and dusted just a few years later, when email took over the world. But I still wonder if anyone out there has an SV88 with the factory-option fax machine fitted.

In this case, the fax machine was a function of its time; but in other cases, car makers still manage to get caught in a time warp that nobody else seems to be trapped in. As late as 1976, Holden found itself with a few hundred HJ two-door coupes lying about, so the decision was made to convert them to HX bodywork, slap on some wheels, decals and ritzy trim, and call them the LE. At the time, the whole combo had parts bin written all over it and the plush burgundy trim was an invitation to snigger. But the real thigh-slapper was the eight-track cartridge stereo the LE sported. Where on earth Holden got a batch of eight-tracks in 1976 is anybody's guess. How exactly it thought an eight-track, years after the cassette became popular, would raise the car's shares is another head-scratcher altogether.

The name and shame game

What's in a name? Plenty, when it comes to placing a giant millstone around a car's neck before it even hits showrooms. Car makers spend millions when it comes to the naming and marketing of their next new model. But even then, it doesn't always turn out well.

You're probably familiar with some of the common naming balls-ups; like the time in the 1970s when Chevrolet named its new compact car the Nova. Only to discover that no-va means 'no go' in Spanish-speaking markets (although, oddly enough, it still sold well). Mitsubishi famously discovered that in some countries and dialects, a Pajero is a person who, er, helps themselves to themselves.

But there have been plenty of others that car makers just didn't see coming. And recently. Take the Jaguar R-Sport, for example. Seems harmless enough. But now say it quickly, and it becomes something else entirely. And imagine the confusion in Ford Australia's boardroom when women of a certain maturity – the very people at whom their new compact SUV was aimed – turned their noses up at a car called the Kuga. Actually, Ford was sipping from the same cup of loony back in the 1990s when it launched a mid-sized coupe called the Cougar – but they had an excuse, because the internet wasn't yet a thing, and nor was any TV program about 'real housewives'. None of which explains Ford's decision to name the

Cougar's predecessor the Probe. Sick puppies.

The other thigh-slapper of recent times was Subaru's all-wheel-drive, mid-sized go-anywhere action wagon. It was called the Levorg which, as anybody who can spell could decipher, is actually Grovel written backwards. Oh dear.

Dishonourable mentions from overseas include the Isuzu Big Horn (no explanation required) and the Fiat 500 Pop, which the crueller among us have suggested accurately described the engine's not-too-distant future.

And we couldn't leave out the Nissan Cedric.

The Cedric was launched in Australia way back in the '60s when, as a nation, we were probably not quite as culturally progressive as we are today. The Q and A session after the technical presentation was dominated by questions about the name of the new Nissan. It was pointed out to the visiting Nissan brass by one of the ever-helpful Aussie journos that the name Cedric was considered locally to have a somewhat homosexual connotation.

'And,' asked the top-ranking Nissan man in the room, 'are there many of these homosexuals in Australia?'

'Oh, thousands,' replied the journo.

'Then we will sell many, many Cedrics,' said Nissan's man.

Touché.

THAT'S NOT A CRASH ...

Anything more than a couple of cars involved in the same crash immediately gets labelled a pile-up. But here in Oz, we're amateurs. The biggest pile-up in history happened in Brazil back in 2011. On a highway in the capital, São Paulo, thick fog caused more than 300 vehicles to plough into each other, leaving a two-kilometre trail of destruction. Perhaps amazingly, only one person was killed and 30 were injured. Just to make sure it made the news, a few of the cars involved even managed to burst into flames.

Ford's V8 returns – with a catch

New Old Stock (NOS) is an automotive industry term to describe components that are old but brand new. Pardon? In other words, bits-and-pieces that were made years and even decades ago, but have never been fitted to a car. So, if you were rummaging around an old petrol station and found an ancient Stromberg carburettor, still in its box and grease-paper, that'd be a great NOS find. But sometimes, NOS parts are sourced direct from the factory – which is exactly what Ford did in the 1990s when it finally decided to reverse its somewhat questionable decision of a decade earlier to drop the V8 option for its Falcon and Fairlane models.

The parts in question were complete V8 engines – a 5.0-litre Windsor V8 – that Ford had stopped building years earlier when a newer, smarter V8 was developed. Ford Oz didn't want the new motor, and instead figured that if it could buy the old Windsors from head office in Detroit at a good price, it could quickly and easily (not to mention, cheaply) bang out a new V8 Falcon for the Ford faithful Down Under. Job done.

So, Ford Oz bought up just about every remaining 5.0-litre Windsor engine left in the world – which wasn't difficult, because about the only industry still interested in the old Windsor was a marine-engine company which was using the thing to turn into inboard boat motors. Certainly, no other car maker was still using the ancient Windsor.

Ford cleared a big corner of its warehouse and piled the unused

... if there's one thing an internal combustion engine doesn't really like doing, it's sitting around doing nothing.

crate engines right up to the roof and started fitting them to cars as the orders came in from dealerships. This was fine for a while; but if there's one thing an internal combustion engine doesn't really like doing, it's sitting around doing nothing. Eventually (as the AU Falcon was starting to use up the last of the stockpiled donks) the situation had become a bit dire. Those old engines, although still technically brand-spankers were, in some cases, starting to develop a bit of surface rust in the cylinder bores. That meant the piston rings could be damaged when the engine was finally started for the first time. If that happened, you had yourself an engine that would burn oil for the whole of its life. Or until it was rebuilt.

By this stage, Ford had its Tickford operation cranking out niche performance models like TE, TS and TL50, and these were expensive cars. Too expensive to be allowed to roll off the end of the production line with an engine that was going to burn oil from day one, anyway. The potential for damage to the Tickford brand was too much to leave to chance. So, for each and every Tickford-badged car with a 5.0-litre V8, Ford took an engine out of the warehouse, disassembled it by hand, carefully honed the bores to remove any rust or rubbish, and then bolted it all back together. Again, by hand.

Exactly what this did to the profitability of these cars is a good question. But it was clearly a big enough impost that the cheaper, Ford-badged XR8 Falcon (which used the same engines from the same corner of the warehouse) didn't get the same degree of love. Instead, V8s were pulled out of stock at random, bolted into cars and sold. If they didn't come back to the dealership with an owner complaining about oil consumption, great. If they did, Ford didn't even bother opening the engine, it just grabbed another one off the pile, stuck that in and crossed its fingers.

The cult of the SUV

Fashion and fads have a lot to answer for. The mullet, neck tatts and the SUV, for starters. Now, I know there are a couple of valid reasons for buying an SUV. They start with the ride height making it easier to strap young 'uns into child restraints, and end with the same feature making it easier for those of us with creaky knees to get in and out. But that's really about it.

Fact is, an SUV is a giant collection of compromises, forced upon us by the desire to look like everybody else. Fashion, in other words.

It all started a few years back when off-road four-wheel drives were flavour of the month. Suddenly, these behemoths started turning up for school runs and grocery-getting duties. This, of course, made no sense to anyone – so, naturally, thousands of us embraced the idea like a long-lost brother. The problem was that these huge vehicles took up a lot of real estate on the road (a lot of them were even too tall to drive into a multi-storey car-park), they used lots and lots of fuel, tyres were expensive, and they were high maintenance.

Part of the mindset was that people wanted to believe that they'd do the big outback adventure one day – even though their definition of roughing it was when the flat-screen in the condo was less than 60 inches across. Deluded they may have been, but they kept buying off-road vehicles and putting up with the many downsides.

The car-park at Uluru. About as close to off-road as most SUVs will ever get.

The solution was to invent the SUV, which kind of looks like it could scale Uluru even though it would never need to. Unfortunately, this turned out to be a marketing-driven solution because, from an engineering point of view, many of the same problems that afflicted off-roaders managed to stick around to haunt SUV owners. Many of them, for instance, still had all-wheel drive (although not the proper off-road type with super-low gear ratios) so they were still heavy and still used plenty of fuel. They were still physically big and tall, and many of them were still a bit of a bus to drive thanks to that bulk and heft.

There were other drawbacks as well. Because the SUV didn't look butch enough until the designers jacked it up, it now needed stiffer springs to control the higher centre of gravity. That sent ride quality down the drain in a lot of cases without completely fixing the issue of body-roll in corners. And if butch is your thing, fine, but most SUVs look like try-hards. Oh, and let's not forget that no matter how rough and tough they look, they aren't actually any good off-road thanks to that lack of low-ratio gears, plus their road-oriented tyres.

Things got truly weird when somebody came up with the idea of

... many of the same problems that afflicted off-roaders managed to stick around to haunt SUV owners.

an SUV that didn't have all-wheel drive of any sort. Suddenly we had all these front-wheel-drive El Butcho vehicles that couldn't go beyond the gravel at little Hamish's pony club car park. And then came downsizing, at which point emerged a new generation of SUVs that were based on little hatchbacks and were completely useless for doing anything remotely outdoors-y. Nobody wants to have to fold their boogie-board in two just to get it into the car.

But still we kidded ourselves. Many people will tell you they bought an SUV for 'the interior space'. They have it all wrong. Thanks to bigger suspension towers and extra driveline components, the packaging of an SUV will usually be tighter than the conventional car on which it's based.

And then there's price. Seriously, go and take a look at the new-car adverts right now. The compact hatchback in a manufacturer's range might typically be priced around the mid-$20s. The SUV spun off that platform? Figure on about a ten-grand price gouge. All for the privilege of driving something with less room, less performance, a greater thirst, more body roll and a harsher ride. So now tell me the whole SUV thing isn't a fad that can't (but won't) disappear fast enough.

As the slimy car-salesman in *National Lampoon's Vacation* said: 'You think you hate it now? Wait 'til you drive it.'

WHICH-A-SIDE?

Crazy though it seems, even into the 1920s, Italy had a pretty loose grasp on the need to drive on a particular side of the road. In cities you drove on the left, and in the countryside, the right. No kidding! Even after the country became a drive-on-the-right nation about 1927, many Italian car buyers still favoured right-hand-drive cars.

The other oddity was Sweden, which started out driving on the left as in Australia, but figured that the left-hand-drive cars it had easiest access to made driving on the right more sensible. Also, its neighbouring countries, Norway and Finland, already drove on the right, so it made all sorts of sense. Even so, the Swedes resisted the move, voting no to a change in a 1955 referendum.

But by the mid '60s it was obvious that change would be for the best so on Sunday, 3 September, 1967, all non-essential traffic was banned from the roads between 1am and 6am. Any vehicles on the road had to come to a complete stop at 4.50am, change to the right-hand side of the road, and re-commence their journeys at 5am. There was even a song by The Telstars to remind people in the run-up to the change, called 'Keep to the Right, Svensson'.

Caught short in unfamiliar Territory

The modern turbo-diesel engine can be a charming thing – provided you can live with the emissions that, science has agreed, are nastier than those of a petrol engine making the same power. But that doesn't alter the effortless flexibility inherent in a good modern turbo-diesel, and it's true that while they're still a bit on the grubby side, their emissions have never been cleaner.

For decades, the high price of fuel in Europe meant that the Continent (and the UK) were very much diesel passenger-car markets. When a litre of diesel could stretch for sometimes double the distance of a litre of petrol, the maths really made sense over there. But it wasn't quite that way here where fuel is generally a lot cheaper and, until about the turn of the century, Australian diesel had huge amounts of sulphur in it.

So much, sulphur, in fact, that car makers such as Mercedes-Benz and BMW refused to sell their diesel-engined models here, knowing the sulphur content would kill the engines. That changed with a revision of the relevant government standards and, suddenly, we were seeing all sorts of exciting new diesel-powered makes and models.

For a while there, diesel was the new black. Even though it wasn't perfect, it was still sexy enough to have buyers flocking to turbo-diesel cars and SUVs. And if you were trying to sell a relatively heavy, full-sized SUV in the first decade of this century and you didn't have a turbo-diesel option, you were pushing it uphill. With a pointy stick.

That was certainly the experience for Ford, which had been selling the very cleverly engineered and designed Territory SUV since 2004, but only with a petrol engine. The four-litre six lifted from the Falcon was certainly a capable powerplant in the Territory, but it soon became obvious that the old girl had quite the thirst. Like a sailor on shore-leave, in fact. So why, asked everybody from motoring journos to Ford dealers to would-be buyers, can't we have a diesel version?

Ford shuffled from one foot to the other, suggesting that the petrol-six Territory was perfect just the way it was. The real truth was that the hold-up was partly the cost of developing and engineering the Territory for a different drivetrain. But it was also true that Ford simply had no go-to turbo-diesel engine that it could pilfer from anywhere else. The mothership in the US was all about petrol engines in anything with fewer than 18 wheels; conversely, Ford's European operation was concentrating on engines much smaller than the one needed to shunt a two-tonne Territory on its way.

It wasn't until Ford somehow became the custodian of the Jaguar and Land Rover brands (that's another story) that a suitable turbo-diesel engine emerged in the form of the 2.7-litre V6 turbo-diesel used in some versions of the Land Rover and Jaguar ranges. Ford Oz set the wheels in motion and rattled off a batch of turbo-diesel Territories for the 2011 model year but, frankly, the moment had passed. Perhaps if Ford had given us a diesel Territory way back in 2004 when diesel really had its mojo on, things might have been different. As it was, it was a case of too little, and even more critically, too late.

The other vehicle that could have made a bigger impact here with a diesel engine was the retro-styled Toyota FJ Cruiser. Based on the Prado off-roader, the FJ clearly could have been engineered for diesel power (as the vast majority of Prados sold here are) but the problem this time was the intended market.

The politics of stupid

See, Australia was just a sideshow for the FJ Cruiser – the main thrust was into the fun-loving North American market where, thanks to seriously cheap (by global standards) fuel, only big rigs and earthmoving equipment have diesel engines. The point being that because nobody in the US would buy a diesel-powered FJ Cruiser, the rest of the world wasn't going to get one either. Given the Prado underpinnings, the engineering would have been a snap, but Toyota just wasn't interested.

Ironically, even though the FJ was aimed squarely at the US, Australian buyers took to the concept much more enthusiastically, even with the lack of a diesel-engine option. In North America, too many buyers passed over the FJ as too cutesy or too small inside to be a proper alternative to a four-wheel-drive pick-up – the default vehicle for middle America. Which is why Toyota, after sinking millions into the project, quietly removed it from US price lists in 2014, just eight years after it was first seen. Thanks to its greater popularity in Australia, the FJ continued here until 2016, but you have to wonder how big it might have been if Toyota had only fitted

No ignition system gives the diesel a big leg-up in river crossings

Diesel is still the choice of outback travellers, too

it with the Prado's well-respected turbo-diesel engine.

Now that diesel is starting to lose its flavour-of-the-month status in Australia and even SUV sales are swinging around to petrol power, it could be argued the Ford Territory and the FJ Cruiser might simply have been cars that were ahead of their time. Which is a mighty big call for, respectively, a heavy and thirsty SUV and a retro-styled off-roader. But that's the car industry for you.

Other diesel-engined clangers to have been perpetrated here amount to a handful of imported hatchbacks and small sedans that have adopted turbo-diesel technology, but failed to incorporate that other Aussie must-have, an automatic transmission. The Mazda3 and Ford Focus, to name just two, were otherwise hot sellers in petrol guise, but the bulk of their sales were the two-pedal version. The root of the problem was that these diesel hatches were usually targeted at the European market where, like diesel engines, the manual transmission is the rule rather than the exception. Unlike in Australia, where pushing a clutch pedal is seen by most drivers as a job requirement worthy of time-and-a-half penalty rates.

NOT SO EFFICIENT

You can always spot the bloke who's just bought a brand-new car. He'll be the one banging on about how efficient the engine is. Thing is, he's probably a bit deluded. Most petrol engines, even modern designs, struggle to beat about 20 or 25 per cent thermal efficiency. Diesels can achieve roughly 40 per cent and a new petrol engine design from Toyota back in 2014 made headlines by offering as much as 38 per cent thermal efficiency. But get this, way back in 1946, the PS *Waverley* paddle boat used an engine that was good for 35 per cent efficiency as it splashed between various bits of Scotland. And what sort of engine did it have? A triple-expansion steam engine. Save that one for the pub.

Toyota LandCruiser – taking the wrong track

Okay, let's start by saying that the first part of this wasn't really Toyota's fault, even if it did affect a lot of Australians. See, Down Under has always been a huge market for the Toyota LandCruiser. After the Middle East, no other market buys more LandCruisers than we do. And that's not in per capita terms; we're talking in outright numbers.

The problem occurred when Toyota moved to a turbo-diesel V8 engine for the LandCruiser 200-Series and its commercial derivatives. There was really nothing wrong with the old turbo-diesel six Toyota had been using for years but, hey, a V8 will always be sexier, right? Exactly. So for 2008, the LandCruiser got the new 4.5-litre, turbo-diesel V8 in a vehicle that wasn't really too much different from the tough-as-nails four-wheel-drive vehicles with which we'd become so familiar.

What was different was that the new engine was physically wider than the old inline six, forcing Toyota to widen the front track to give the new V8 somewhere to physically sit and still be able to close the bonnet. In other words, the front wheels of the 'Cruiser were now further apart.

Now, that mightn't sound like a huge issue and, on bitumen, it wasn't. But you need to remember that such was the omnipresence of the Toyota puddle-jumper in rural Australia over the decades that just about every off-road track anywhere had been forged by a million previous LandCruisers. Suddenly, your spanking new 'Cruiser

The very first LandCruiser and the one the purists reckon was the best ever – the 80 Series. Between them, they made just about every bush track in this country.

didn't sit in the same wheel tracks, so it might be harder work getting down the track to your favourite campsite. Even on a familiar track, there could now be a rock or a tree stump right where you want to put a wheel.

Like I said, there wasn't much Toyota could do about that; but the second part of the story is definitely down to Toyota. Or, more likely, to Toyota's accounts department. Because even though the front track was now wider, Toyota didn't make the rear track wider by the same amount. In fact, it wasn't any wider at all. Now the front wheels of the Toyota didn't want to follow the old tracks, and the rear wheels didn't want to follow the fronts, preferring instead to fall into the original ruts created by the ghosts of LandCruisers past.

This wasn't usually a deal-breaker, but it did prove that no vehicle is perfect. Especially not once you've let the bean-counters call any of the shots.

The other infamous example of a wider engine diminishing a car was in the 1970s, when Jaguar switched the classic DOHC six cylinder engine for a V12 in its iconic E-Type model. The wider V12 meant the front wheels had to be pushed out, and that meant the previously svelte E-Type now sported an ugly set of flared wheel-arches. This, on an original design that Enzo Ferrari himself had proclaimed the most beautiful car ever made. Adding insult to cosmetic injury, the V12 was more complicated, less reliable, thirstier and didn't actually go any harder than the original six. D'oh!

LEFTY LOOSEY, RIGHTY TIGHTY

Ever seen someone struggling to undo the wheel nuts on an old Valiant? If the wheel is on the left-hand side, it could well be that the poor sod is actually tightening them. Valiants used left-hand-threaded wheel nuts well into the 1960s, but only on the left side. The theory was that the normal rotation of the wheel would apply a tightening force to the left-hand nuts. Globally, Mopar brands (but there were others, too) were very keen on this practice. Thing is, I don't recall wheels constantly falling off cars without this feature. And how many studs were broken off by hapless owners thinking they had a seized wheel-nut and going for the big breaker bar?

But getting back to Toyota, the wider track wasn't Toyota's first faux pas as far as LandCruiser owners were concerned. For decades, the 'Cruiser had used a six-stud wheel, which became more-or-less a universal fitment across the four-wheel-drive world. The smart thing to do was to make sure that your off-road trailer, camper or caravan used the same wheels, so that you didn't have to carry two types of spare tyre; one spare would work on either. (Although, as any outback traveller will tell you, one spare tyre is not enough and having two spares is the bare minimum).

The problems started when some versions of the 100 Series LandCruiser went to a five-stud wheel. The mathematics are pretty simple; a car with 20 wheel studs requiring 20 wheel nuts is cheaper to make than the same car with 24 of each. Only now, the new LandCruiser wheels were no longer interchangeable with the ones on their trailers and campers.

It doesn't sound like a big deal on paper; but when most touring four-wheel drives towing a van or camper are loaded to the hilt, having to cart four spare tyres instead of two was a big old pain in the proverbial.

… such was the omnipresence of the Toyota puddle-jumper in rural Australia over the decades that just about every off-road track anywhere had been forged by a million previous LandCruisers.

The day our car industry died

On the afternoon of Friday, 20 October in 2017, the last production car to ever be built in Australia rolled off Holden's Adelaide line. And then everyone went home. For the last time.

Impossible though it seemed, the days of Australia making its own cars were gone, killed off in large part by a federal government that was no longer interested in propping up the industry and the tens of thousands of jobs it represented. It's easy to stand back and say any industry that can't stand on its own two feet deserves to be put to the sword, and that's precisely what the Abbott Coalition government did in 2013 when it refused to extend financial support to the three remaining Aussie car makers – Holden, Ford and Toyota.

But there are a few problems with this. The first is that the initial savings generated by not handing over money to the car industry are very likely to be completely gobbled up by the dole queues that are a dead-set certainty in cases like this. Because we're not talking a handful of jobs here. No, the numbers are frightening.

As many as 5000 workers were directly employed by Holden, Ford and Toyota, and the vast majority of them were out of a job when each manufacturer shut its doors over a 12-month period. But you also need to factor in the little company of a dozen workers in a country town that makes the clips that hold the brake line to the car's body. And every other little company like it, including those employed in retailing and transporting the finished cars. Figure on about 120 suppliers and 50,000 workers across the whole industry, and you're probably getting close.

The problem faced by the car industry in the lead-up to this upheaval was that if just one of the three car manufacturers went, those little component manufacturers who supplied all three brands suddenly lacked the volumes they needed to remain viable. So, once Ford shut up shop for the last time in late 2016, the writing was on the wall for the everybody else.

But here's the terrible reality: the local car makers were lobbying for just $300 million a year over 10 years from the government in industry assistance. That was already less than they'd been receiving up to 2013 when all the cards were laid on the table. And it gets worse: those same car makers had pledged to invest three of their own dollars for every government dollar in assistance.

It's important to note, too, that there isn't a single car-making nation that doesn't prop up its industry financially or through protectionism, or both. Not one. So Australia was hardly the odd man out in terms of needing a leg-up to keep the cars rolling off the line, and its workers out of Centrelink.

Let's not forget that the local Feds cream off about $500 million a year in luxury car tax, so they could have agreed on an assistance package and still had change left over. And now that there's no need to protect an industry that no longer exists, there are calls from many quarters to axe the luxury car tax. Talk about shooting yourself in the foot.

Here's the other terrible truth: until 2017, Australia was one of about 13 countries in the world that could design, engineer and build a car from scratch. And now it's not. Many of Ford's best and brightest have taken up positions in Silicon Valley in the US, and that brain-drain is set to continue as talented Australian engineers and designers seek their fortune elsewhere. Your government at work. Thanks for nothing.

Not just us

WHERE IT'S GONE WRONG IN THE REST OF THE WORLD

Off the pace from the get-go

Depending how you looked at it, the AMC Pacer of 1975 was either way ahead of its time or just a whole collection of wrong. It certainly helped hasten the demise of the parent company, American Motors Corporation, and has gone on to become either a '70s design icon or the butt of some cruel jokes. Or both.

There was nothing wrong with the basic concept of a small (by North American standards) car that even incorporated a hatchback at a time when this was still a very novel layout. Even then, the Americans couldn't help themselves and although the Pacer was a solid four-and-a-half feet (140cm) shorter than a Cadillac of the same period, it was within two inches (5cm) of being as wide.

The problems started arriving towards the end of the Pacer's design phase. The plan all along had been to use a Wankel rotary engine, built by General Motors and supplied to AMC. But as GM found (and Mazda and NSU both found out the hard way) the rotary was a tricky beast to get right. So just a few months before the Pacer entered production, GM announced it wouldn't be building the rotary after all. It was just too hard to get the thing to hang together, and controlling its thirst for oil and petrol was another matter entirely. That left AMC between a rock and a hard place, so the Pacer (which had allegedly already swallowed more than $50 million in design and development costs) was hastily re-engineered to accept an existing AMC engine. Which turned out to be a huge, high and long inline six-cylinder.

The packaging was appalling, with the last couple of cylinders tucked up under the lower edge of the windscreen. That made even a simple job like changing a rocker-cover gasket a major headache. The big engine also robbed the Pacer of any real fuel economy advantage over the opposition, although experience suggests it wouldn't have been much different (if at all) with a rotary engine on board.

Despite all that, the Pacer sold really well. Initially. With 145,000 sales in the first year, things were looking good. But by then, as observers have put it, everybody who wanted a Pacer had one. Sales tanked. It was also about then that the quality problems started showing up. Those huge glass areas (37 per cent of the car's body area) let in bulk amounts of UV radiation, which toasted interiors quick smart. The engines also leaked oil, the electronic ignition gave trouble, the brakes were poor and the suspension crude.

The fuel economy thing haunted the Pacer, too, combined with fuel shortages and safety concerns about the roof crushing in a rollover. That led AMC to use thicker metal panels, which had the unintended consequence of increasing the weight and hurting fuel consumption even more. By the late '70s, it was clear the Pacer had run its course. With AMC bleeding money from various wounds, the axe finally fell with production stopping in 1979 and the last sales occurring in 1980.

The car is now seen as part of the AMC downfall, and the corporation was bought out just a handful of years later by Chrysler – mainly to get its hands on the potentially very lucrative Jeep division, which AMC also owned at that stage. The Jeep brand has since gone on to some great things. And the Pacer's finest moment? Without a doubt, its cameo in the 1992 blockbuster comedy *Wayne's World*.

AMC's Pacer should have been a winner, in theory. The watered-down production version was, um, not.

Dieselgate

It was September 2015 and the automotive juggernaut that is the Frankfurt Motor Show was in full swing. I was there as a guest of Audi, a part of the Volkswagen Group, so I attended the huge VW family show-and-tell night in a gigantic (and full) stadium. Everyone from VW group boss Martin Winterkorn to the heads of each group company was there, performing mic-drops and spouting info and glimpses of what was to come in terms of new product. Yep, it was a real upbeat show.

What we didn't know at the time, though, was that the scheisse was about to hit the fan in the biggest way ever seen in the car industry. There would be sackings, jailings, billions of dollars in fines issued, millions of disgruntled customers all over the world, and years and years of fallout to follow.

Yep, Dieselgate dropped. In fact, it all turned to crap while I was on the plane back to Australia. Had we journos known what was about to happen, we'd doubtless have been told to stay put in Germany and start asking tough questions. Certainly, the questions asked at the VW Family love-in would have been very different ones.

In any case, the Dieselgate fiasco would generate billions of column-centimetres of copy for newspapers, magazines and websites of the world, and not just the motoring titles. Here was one of the biggest, proudest companies in the world, caught with its pants down, cheating on official

Diesel already stank, but when VW was finished with it, the stuff was really on the nose

exhaust emission tests. It's difficult to overstate just what a scandal this was.

So – what did they do, and how did they do it?

The idea is actually quite brilliant. You design a car that can differentiate between normal driving in the real world, and when it's being tested for its tailpipe emissions. Fundamentally, various diesel-powered makes and models of VW Group cars (including Audi, Skoda and Porsche) were fitted with software that could make this distinction. So, when the car was placed on an emissions testing rig, it detected as much and engaged a set of engine-management protocols to reduce its emissions below the legal requirement. Bingo – test passed.

When the car sensed it was being driven in the real world, it reverted to a set of management tables to make more power and potentially use less fuel. But its tailpipe emissions went through the roof – in some cases, to as much as 40 times the legal limit.

But how did it do it? The car's on-board computer looked at what was going on to determine whether it was being tested or not. That included taking note of steering inputs (the car doesn't need to be steered on a test rig). If no steering inputs were

Not just us

detected, the car determined it was on a dyno or test rig and would then alter the way the engine's exhaust gas recirculation valves worked. These valves are used to force the engine to consume a portion of its own exhaust to clean up emissions; but if the computer bypasses it, performance increases and fuel consumption can be reduced, but emissions of oxides of nitrogen sky-rocket.

In the months leading up to the bombshell, I had heard some of VW's competitors privately asking how on earth VW managed to produce diesel engines that could generate so much performance, use so little fuel and yet still pass the sniff test. It seems those other car makers weren't the only ones scratching their heads. In 2014, the year before the headlines hit, a clean-air council in the US performed some real-world tests on VW diesel cars. And what they found was the start of the whole thing. Regardless of what VW was claiming, the tests showed the cars were producing vastly more tailpipe emissions than they should have been. Suddenly, alarm bells started sounding all over the place.

When the Dieselgate storm hit, it caught most people – including the

Volkswagen's diesel engines had even the competition wondering how they did it. Now we know. Oops.

VW head honcho, Martin Winterkorn – one of many victims of Dieselgate

German government – off balance. But it was immediately obvious this was a big deal, and nothing would ever be the same again. Within days, Martin Winterkorn – the bloke who had been spruiking the family's brands just days earlier in that Frankfurt basketball stadium – had fallen on his sword. Mind you, he didn't have much choice with the sheer number of blow-torches being pointed at his arse.

Component maker Bosch was dragged into the mess, with suggestions it had played a part in developing the cheat device. Bosch denied any complicity. A German newspaper report at the time suggested Bosch had known about VW's plans, and had issued a written warning that fitting the software was not cricket and that VW had been cheating on emissions tests in this way since 2005.

By October 2015, Dieselgate had gone global as all markets that VW operated in, including Australia, took a close look at what was going on. Finally, VW could stonewall no longer and admitted it had fitted the cheat devices way back in 2008. At that point in proceedings, VW issued a recall for 8.5 million cars in Europe and admitted it had sold dodgy cars in China. US VW boss Michael Horn admitted he had known since 2014 that the devices were being fitted. The lawsuits, class-actions and fines started flooding in.

Meantime, VW sales start to tank around the world and the company said it would suspend production in several of its plants. Deals started getting done in different countries to try to sort out the mess. Owners of affected cars expressed concern that their wonderful performance and fuel economy – which attracted them to a Volkswagen in the first place - would be affected once the iffy software had been removed. They had a point.

By the start of 2016, no lesser body than the US Justice Department had weighed in, suing VW, Audi and Porsche over the cheat devices and for violating climate protection regulations (no irony there). Yet VW was stonewalling again, claiming the violation had been the result of a 'mistake the company's engineers had not been aware of'.

In April 2016, VW reportedly had set aside 16.2 billion euros (approximately $AUD 26 billion) to pay for compensation and fines, a move contrasted by the decision to cut the

Not just us

bonuses of its managers by 30 per cent. But only temporarily. Ultimately, the compensation payouts are expected to be much higher, but it's the other fallout that is likely to be longer lasting.

Part of that is the damage to VW's image. Mind you, despite the whole Dieselgate wrangle, VW still managed to build 10.3 million cars in 2016, making it the world's biggest car maker. But there are still plenty of consumers who won't forgive VW for the fiasco, and have sworn off the products for good. It's also possible the money VW had to put aside for make-goods has put the brakes on its new-model development. For the last decade or so, VW's products have been a good generation farther down the evolutionary track than the majority of its competitors (which is why they sold so well) so the financial hit will give those competitors a chance to play catch-up and reduce or eliminate that development shortfall.

Back in 2015, VW had just bought motorcycle brand Ducati and was working on some really interesting crossover vehicles using Ducati engines. In fact, one of them was shown at that 2015 Frankfurt Motor Show. Suddenly, all that peripheral stuff got taken out the back and shot as VW bunkered down for the fight of its life. Reports suggested Ducati was back on the market, Audi was yanked out of endurance racing, and diesel passenger cars were on the nose.

In fact, the scandal has probably accelerated the demise of diesel for anything smaller than trucks and buses as governments and lobby groups grow tired of the emissions and the damage they can cause. On the upside, the early death of diesel has probably pulled forward the development of hybrid and electric vehicles. So if there's any silver lining to the global cock-up that was Dieselgate, that'll be it.

Owners of affected cars expressed concern that their wonderful performance and fuel economy ... would be affected once the iffy software had been removed. They had a point.

Lives versus profits

Ford's US-market Pinto was quite a departure for the Blue Oval. It was the first time the brand got serious about a more compact car that would use less fuel than the full-sized barges it was selling at the same time. But in other ways – namely, the way Ford (and other brands) viewed personal safety – the Pinto was more of the same.

A series of design problems early in the Pinto's life led to a spate of post-crash fires that injured and killed many people. In fact, within a year or so of the car's launch in 1970, reports of the first casualties were coming in. It was scary stuff: even a low-speed, rear-end impact could be enough to turn a Pinto into a fireball. These were accidents in which the occupants weren't hurt in the crash, but burned to death in the ensuing fire.

So what was the problem? Well, there were many, starting with a rear bumper that was largely decorative rather than offering any sort of crash barrier. Then there was the placement of the fuel tank between the so-called bumper and the rear axle (a common arrangement in other makes) and a series of weak joints where the filler neck joined the tank. Throw in a layout that could see the tank pierced by the differential bolts or the rear shock absorbers, and you had all the ingredients for a post-shunt fire.

Independent crash-lab testing soon showed up the problems, and a range of potential fixes were suggested. One was to fit a metal plate between the bumper and the fuel tank. This was reckoned at the time to cost $11 per car. A rubber bladder inside the fuel tank, to contain the contents if the metal outer was ruptured, would cost $5.08 per car. And the third proposal was to fit a plastic buffer to the differential to stop the bolts rupturing the tank. Estimated cost: less than a buck a car.

So which way did Ford jump? Well, this is the disgraceful part, because instead of ponying up for any of these engineering-led fixes, Ford brought in the lawyers and accountants. The brains trust came up with a projected figure of 180 deaths and 180 serious burns, then reached for the calculator. In the end, Ford's figures suggested paying out damages to those victims would cost around $49 million, while recalling and fixing the Pinto would be closer to $137 million. So it did nothing.

The mistake Ford made (aside from moral corruptness in their response to the problem) was to put these calculations on paper in a memo. That memo was eventually discovered, and that's when the courts that were handing out damages to Pinto victims suddenly got medieval on Ford's corporate arse. Courts eventually awarded far more than $137 million, and that sent Ford's lawyers into another frenzy as they desperately started trying to settle cases out of court.

Finally, in 1978, Ford was shamed into recalling all Pintos and retro-fitting them with a stronger fuel-filler neck as well as the plastic guard over the differential bolts. These moves undoubtedly saved lives, but Ford's ethics were called into serious question.

The thought of a corporate citizen stooping to such lows is what made the whole Pinto episode so reprehensible. But you can bet your bottom dollar it wasn't the first time that big business had put profits before humanity. Nor, undoubtedly, was it the last.

Throw another supercar on the barbie

The Lamborghini Miura is often credited as the seminal modern supercar. With its mid-mounted V12 engine, two-seater layout and movie-star looks, the Miura cast the mould for pretty much every supercar that followed it. Trust me, in 1966, this thing was sex on Pirellis. But it soon developed a reputation for being hot stuff in other ways. Mainly as a fire trap. Lamborghini insisted on using four three-barrel carburettors for the Miura. Which would be fine, but the carbs it chose were downdraught Webers that were more of a race carburettor than something suitable for a road car.

The problems started when the car was idled even for a short time, and then the throttles snapped open – say, when taking off from a red light. (Actually, the fact that no self-respecting Miura driver in the 1960s would ever have stopped for a red light should have solved the problem). When the throttles opened, the carbs sprayed a mist of fuel into the engine bay where it would very likely (thanks to the layout of the carburettors and ignition) come into contact with the spark plugs and the mighty ignition system powering the 12 cylinders. The same thing could happen when a hot motor was restarted. The results were inevitable. Is it a coincidence that Weber is also a brand of barbecue?

Fast-forward a handful of years, and the typical Latin approach to maintenance often resulted in Miuras sporting leaky fuel lines and worn carburettor internals, all of which only

All Lambos are hot-rods; the Miura was a little toastier than most

made the problem worse. Even today, when any still-surviving Miura has been restored to a state of perfection, the advice from owners is to try not to stop the car and restart a hot engine (when refuelling, for example). In fact, some experts reckon modern fuel with any alcohol content has a lower boiling point than old-school leaded fuel, and is therefore even more likely to boil and bubble up through the carbs during a short stop-and-restart sequence.

The key piece of advice for modern-day Miura owners? Keep an extinguisher handy and know how to use it.

WHY PLASTIC?

Ever wondered why the Chev Corvette uses a fibreglass body over a steel frame? Seems like a strange way to go in the US in the '50s, right? Well, it seems the plastic-over-steel method was used to produce a prototype (it was simpler) and that car was accidentally crashed. But it survived so well, the decision was made to enter production using the same techniques. So I'm told.

The 'safety' device that could kill you

Let's talk irony: the Takata airbag. Yep, it's a safety device that could kill you. As paradoxes go, it's up there with the best. The mandatory recall of up to 2.3 million Aussie cars as a result of the fiasco is proof that illogical doesn't always equal funny. And that's just in Australia; the number of affected cars in the US is reckoned to be 42 million.

The Australian federal government's move to make the safety recall a mandatory (rather than voluntary) one in 2018 underlined the seriousness of the situation. The Feds had never done this before, instead relying on the car companies to get their house in order whenever there's been a safety issue. But this time, there was just too much at stake. After trying an initial voluntary recall for affected vehicles, the subsequent head-count revealed that as many as a million cars on Australian roads had fallen through the net and had not had their driver and passenger airbags replaced. So Canberra acted.

Mind you, the government hasn't been too quick out of the blocks considering the first death chalked up to a Takata airbag occurred in the US back in 2009. The first Australian death was in 2017 when a Sydney man driving a Honda had a crash. But it wasn't the actual crash that killed him; it was the carnage inflicted when the airbag deployed incorrectly and with far too much violence. So far it's reckoned that, globally, as many as 22 deaths and 230 serious injuries have been caused by these airbags.

Closer to home, the fiasco has meant that there are more than a million cars on the road right now that have the potential to kill you in even a minor crash.

Now, if you've ever seen an airbag go off, you'll know that it's an inherently violent procedure. In fact, it's a controlled explosion, so it's never going to be pretty. So what's different about these Takata 'bags? Well, to start with, all airbags use ammonium nitrate as the explosive. But – and it's a big but – the conventional wisdom is that you also add a second chemical, to act as a stabilising agent. Takata didn't do that with the airbags in question.

In humid climates (like large parts of Australia, for instance) moisture can migrate into the ammonium nitrate charge and cause it to behave differently when it's triggered. Apparently, the stabilising chemical would prevent that – but that's academic at this point. When that happens, the airbag explodes with way more force than it should. Enough force that it's capable of causing the metal canister containing the charge to be torn apart and ejected with the airbag. And it's the metal shrapnel from this canister that has lethal potential.

An airbag manufacturer since 1980, Takata has now declared bankruptcy (surprise, surprise) but even so, it's facing tens of billions of dollars' worth of injury claims, not to mention legal costs. Closer to home, the fiasco has meant that there are more than a million cars on the road right now that have the potential to kill you in even a minor crash. And there are car owners out there who still don't seem to understand that their car could become a lethal weapon in even a minor shunt.

About the author

The car is a complex machine. The business of making cars is a complex industry. Enter a simple man.

Dave Morley has been an automotive journalist for the last three decades and more, and has witnessed firsthand his fair share of mistakes, errors, cock-ups and bald-faced lies from a car-making world where, too often, politics, expediency, cost-cutting, and snake-oil salesmen get in the way of good design, best practice and engineering practicalities. How else could you explain a manufacturer cheating on a fuel consumption test, a car that knee-capped its occupants or an exhaust design so loopy it set the car's carpets on fire?

If it has wheels and an engine, it can go wrong. Anywhere, anytime.

A twisted view of the world isn't usually a blessing, but when it comes to stripping away the weasel words and recognising stupid for what it is, such a warped approach has served Dave well.

Acknowledgements

Try to remember the hundred daftest/craziest/most unlikely things you've seen in a 30 or 40 year career and I bet you'd need help, too. So here's a list of the people who sat down with me, ripped the lid off a beer and cast their minds back to recall the individual events that make up this book. They know who they are, and now, so do you.

Guy Allen
Rob Blackbourn
Marc Bondini
Sean Bondini
Andrew Britten
Tim Britten
Peter Hickey
Nathan Jacobs
Graeme Lewis
Ernest Litera
Tim Mattison
Stuart Morley
Paul Newbold
Mat Raudonikis
Grant Roff
Glenn Torrens

Published in 2019 by Hardie Grant Travel, a division of Hardie Grant Publishing

Hardie Grant Travel (Melbourne)
Building 1, 658 Church Street
Richmond, Victoria 3121

Hardie Grant Travel (Sydney)
Level 7, 45 Jones Street
Ultimo, NSW 2007

www.hardiegrant.com/au/travel

Explore Australia is an imprint of Hardie Grant Travel

A catalogue record for this book is available from the National Library of Australia

Great Aussie Car Fails
ISBN 9781741176735

10 9 8 7 6 5 4 3 2 1

Publisher
Melissa Kayser
Project editor
Megan Cuthbert
Editor
Steve Colquhuon
Proofreader
Susan Keogh
Design
Neighbourhood Creative
Typesetting
Kerry Cooke
Prepress
Kerry Cooke and Splitting Image Colour Studio

Printed and bound in China by LEO Paper Group